Fascism and the Women's Cause

Fascism and the Women's Cause

Alex Charnley and Michael Richmond

Ebb

First published 2025
© 2025 Ebb Books

The right of Alex Charnley and Michael Richmond to be identified as the authors of this Work has been asserted in accordance with sections 77 and 78 of the Copyright, Designs and Patents Act 1988.

Ebb Books, 54 The Oval, Rose Hill, Oxford, OX4 4SE

PB ISBN: 9781738468737
EB ISBN: 9781738468720

British Library Cataloguing-in-Publication Data
A catalogue record for this book is available from the British library.

Typeset in Dante

ebb-books.com

Front cover artwork Christina Broom, 'Suffragettes in Hyde Park' 1908

Contents

Introduction

What if certain forms of feminism, historically, have not simply colluded with white-supremacist projects but have actually been fascist themselves? How might ceasing to deny that
feminisms can be fascist actually strengthen antifascist organizing in this moment?

Sophie Lewis and Asa Seresin, *Fascist Feminism: A Dialogue*[1]

It is now common to see fascists supporting 'gender critical'[2]
(GC) movements, both online and in the streets. Whether this
support is rebuked, ignored, or welcomed, the convergence between gender criticals – only some of whom identify as feminists
but all of whom claim to be fighting for women's rights – and far
right and fascist actors is plain to see. The *Trans Safety Network*
(*TSN*) have reported growing 'practical crossovers' between gender critical movements and the traditional far right, with transphobia acting as a funnel for the latter.[3] As Mallory Moore shows
in her chronology of the term 'gender ideology', Catholic organisations in the early 2010s were first to aggressively push this
term as a warning against feminism. In 2014, the far right used it
as an organising point for anti-feminism. 2016, Moore argues, 'is
the year that this conservative conspiracy theory is adopted by
ostensible feminists.' A significant flashpoint in 2016 was when
'the British Government issued a proposal to review the Gender
Recognition Act with a view to "improving transgender equality."' Moore compiles a chronograph of 'gender panics' to show
how this floating signifier evolved before finally exploding into a
cacophony. As she writes, 'I've had to stop adding in every single
reference from August 15th [2016] onwards, there are simply too
many.'[4] Antisemitic conspiracism has also merged with respectable 'gender critical' transphobia. As Joaquina explains, writing

for *TSN*, 'this transphobic paranoid style is bound by a distinctive common thread: its portrayal of trans people as an inherently deviant, predatory and deadly presence, and a menace to the safety and purity of the young.' Respectable 'gender critical' transphobia and fascist conspiracism are distinguishable only by degree:

> Even before the far-right began focusing on a horror-themed transphobia, it was gender critical ideologues – with their talk of 'child sacrifice' by a trans 'blood cult' and equating trans inclusion to legalising sex crimes – whose rhetoric has echoed a much more vicious strand of antisemitism.[5]

The primacy of transphobia, antisemitism, and Islamophobia in recent conspiracies of civilisational decline have been the means for fascism to pick itself up and re-engage the old myths. Far right groups now organise around 'grooming' narratives as a matter of course, whether against trans and queer people or Asian/Muslim/Pakistani men. And gender critical women are often organising alongside fascists. The instrumentalisation of women's rights issues and the agency of women is central to the contemporary fascist conjuncture. Women have been present, and in leading roles, in Britain's hard right government and Britain's far right parties. This includes some women of colour, able to contrive stereotypes from white feminist traditions to launch racist and transphobic attacks. Suella Braverman, Home Secretary from 2022 to 2023, personifies the tendency: 'I suppose the ethnicity of grooming gang perpetrators in a string of cases is the sort of fact that has simply become unfashionable in some quarters, like the fact that 100% of women do not have a penis.'[6]

This incitement should not be understood as the consequence of a recent coarsening of the public sphere, or as a form of 'distraction' limited to the extreme right. Braverman should be taken seriously on her own terms, but Islamophobia and transmisogyny are entrenched structures of violence. As Ella Cockbain and Waqas Tufail have argued, racist media framings of child sexual exploitation cases that centred on 'Muslim' or 'Asian' 'grooming gangs' developed over a decade ago in Britain. The mainstream circulation of the term 'grooming' became a journalistic shorthand that was normalised in public debate and defended in social policy literature, despite having no basis in 'established legal or social scientific categories.' As Cockbain and Tufail write, 'a relatively small number of high-profile "grooming gangs" cases have been used to claim an 'epidemic' of abuse.'[7] These cases dominated public debate from 2011 onwards and brought many liberal progressives into the fold. Sarah Champion, a Labour MP who was shadow secretary for women and equalities at the time, defended the racialised focus, writing for *The Sun* newspaper in 2017: 'These people are predators, and the common denominator is their ethnic heritage.'[8] This racist emphasis on the vulnerability of white women and girls was reciprocated on the far right. 'Far-right propaganda text *Easy Meat*,' note Cockbain and Tufail, 'features familiar claims about the "epidemic of child-rape by grooming gangs", failed multiculturalism, politically-correct cover-ups and the "collusion" and collective responsibility of "the Muslim community."'[9] The utility of the term 'grooming' was its power of connotation, helping to reshape and reboot racial stereotypes, just as 'mugging' did in the 1970s.[10]

New Labour provided Tories with a template for Islamophobic discourses. Concerns for 'women and young girls' and the fate of the family have now become the lexicon of national conservatism. Manufactured social media rumours of asylum seekers 'following young girls' were used to incite violence against refugees in Knowsley and elsewhere in Britain during a wave of 'whiteness riots' in 2023. Women attended and often led protests at asylum seeker accommodations in Cannock.[11] Ireland too has seen increasing anti-refugee and anti-immigration activity, bringing together far right Irish nationalists and British loyalists, with women videoing themselves confronting suspected migrants.[12] In both countries the same social media tactic gets reproduced, with 'grooming' rumours circulated at targeted locations. In South London, in 2023, this same tactic drew gender critical activists and fascists into a shared calendar of eliminationist anti-trans rallies. Transphobic street rallies were organised against drag queen storytime events in Honor Oak by Turning Point UK (TPUK), alongside other far right and neo-fascist groups.[13] Nick Tenconi, chief operating officer, arrived with a group of men at 5am on Saturday 24th June, alongside neo-Nazis like Lance Wright, a former member of Blood & Honour and Combat 18. These men attacked counter protesters, along with journalist Jess O'Thomson who reported from the scene, 'Tenconi was enthusiastically involved in the street violence, personally offering to fight individuals, and physically moving towards and grabbing at counter-protesters. This is evidence of a clear turn by TPUK towards unapologetic street fascism.'[14] Honor Oak was a 'cis-riot' that functioned similarly to how the 'racist riot' or 'whiteness riot' has historically functioned for the British state. The whiteness riot is not a 'lone' or 'fringe' action. Indeed, in previous work we define the whiteness riot 'as *bordering*, an action that seeks to further incite and lobby for state violence further up the chain.'[15] TPUK functions similarly: to lobby for cisnormativity from the street. This violence becomes a relay for the media to construct a 'parental concern' that the state could act on.

Civilization ending

The historian Jules Gill-Peterson provides a lucid introduction to the colonial origins of the modern 'gender panic'. Focusing on the hijra in Northwestern colonial India, Gill-Peterson writes, 'Sexual immorality was, crucially, interpreted as a political threat to colonial rule… The idea that hijras were male prostitutes with a secret government became the pretext for a statewide campaign to secure moral order by exterminating them.'[16] The hijra were not trans women, but they were 'trans-feminised' by colonial legislation because there was no identity assigned to them. 'Hijras, for one thing, are arguably much older than the Western concept of gender through which trans emerged as boundary crossing.'[17] Gender nonconformity is the more obvious reality for people historically. What the 'cis identity' describes is a *political alignment* that people have been historically recruited into.

Cisnormativity is subject to varied and popular challenges from people whose ordinary life refutes category standards of gender and legal sex. Fascist street movements respond by policing and enforcing standards of 'cisness' and incentivising media and policy debates that strengthen that alignment.[18] Gill-Peterson writes,

> To hate or dislike trans women, to exclude them, or to attack and scorn trans femininity are all anxious attempts to establish a boundary that violence itself admits never existed in the first place. The trans misogynist constantly confesses her, his, or their inability to escape being in the world with trans women and trans femininity by wishing they could enforce segregation. That's why trans-misogynist violence is so often cruel or subservient to despotic authority.[19]

A similar dynamic is at play in the US where fears of gender critical pundits and the fears of the far right reinforce one another. Women have been instrumental to the rise of the far right, from the Tea Party to pro-Trump movements, with significant numbers taking part in 'Stop the Steal' efforts and the January 6 Capitol Insurrection.[20] Women have been particularly active in QAnon networks, moved by calls to #SaveTheChildren. Instagram influencers and suburban moms as well as lifestyle, parenting and wellness bloggers have contributed to the explosion of the conspiracy theory,[21] which accelerated during the pandemic. In an article analysing the trend Gill-Peterson documents the 'key mechanics of the growing relation of gender-critical punditry to QAnon.' A wave of anti-trans bills from 2021 began to 'openly legislate through the specifically conspiratorial language of the QAnon anti-trans platform.' At the respectable end of public debate gender critical pundits raised the alarm about 'trans tipping points' and 'social contagion' among younger generations. Gill-Peterson writes compellingly about 'the appeal to free speech in anti-trans punditry' and what she calls an 'intensely-avowed emotional attachment to liberalism in this genre of complaint.' As she notes, 'what strikes me is not so much the appeal itself [to liberalism] but its appearance within a much wider illiberal field of anti-trans discourse that these figures claim not to endorse.'[22] Centrism appears as a defence of liberal democratic values and moderation of political extremes. But just as the show dog at Crufts must sacrifice all doglike traits to become a marvel of rational design, the centrist rationalises away every liberal trait to become the show dog of liberalism. The triangulating structure of liberal democracy means political appearances are mutable and do not coincide with any stable ideological programme. Gill-Peterson concludes:

> Anti-trans movements demonstrate that conspiracy and disinformation are not outside of, but rather are central to, liberal political institutions. Indeed, anti-trans speech is increasingly the very means by which to launder extremism and conspiracy theory into democratic institutions, with disastrous results.[23]

Gender critical feminism may not be a typical fascist formation, but it is a social movement organised around an eliminationist goal that has managed to influence the state in a way that many fascist groups have historically failed to do. For this reason, the fascist question is being urgently revised by feminists to consider how 'women and girls' advocacy is used to demonise trans people, attack gender nonconformity more broadly, supplement racial as well as gender panic, and legislate against equal rights. This means placing fascism and feminism – often thought of as opposites – in conversation. Yet such an analysis will understandably produce ambiguities and consternation. Serena Bassi and Greta LaFleur introduced a 2022 issue of *Transgender Studies Quarterly* (*TSQ*), asking why 'critiques of how feminism has, today and in earlier times, been invoked in service of a wide range of pernicious and anti-liberationist ends have somehow not yet spurred a careful enough reckoning with the enduringly ambivalent character of feminism.'[24] Enzo Traverso's conceptualisation of 'postfascism' is used to examine continuities and differences between classical modes of historical fascism, neo-fascism and the developing bonds between far right and transphobic groups today.[25] As Bassi and LaFleur write,

> The 'post' in Traverso's 'postfascism' should be read neither
> temporally (as a straightforward aftermath of historical fas-
> cism), nor as negating any kind of world-historical frame,
> but rather as drawing out the entrenched 'fascist potential'
> in supposedly democratic presents... [T]the gender-critical
> politicization of a true womanhood under threat by trans
> politics is not only genealogically coherent with multiple
> conservative moral panics and resilient fascist tropes but also
> with the longue durée of liberal, bourgeois, white feminist
> exclusions perpetrated along racial and class lines.[26]

Traverso conceives of 'postfascism' as a 'particular regime of his-
toricity' following the 'defeat of the revolutions of the twentieth
century' that forced Western far right and neo-fascist parties to
regroup.[27] These groups were forced to consider a conditional
affiliation with liberal democracy after the Cold War, be that
discursively, through a distancing of neo-fascist rhetoric and an
embrace of national electoral rules and formats, or through the
assimilation of neo-fascist memberships and groups into mainstream parties.[28] Fascists are now aware that they cannot *appear*
how they have historically (where they do, they are often marginalised), but the most aggressive, eliminationist postures of gender critical feminism maintain a semblance of innocence based
on the fact that they *seem* to squarely contradict the appearance
of historical fascism. Such ambivalence is exemplified by the persona constructions of Kellie-Jay Keen-Minshull (known as Posie
Parker) who has garnered a significant online audience for her
transphobic rants, calls for armed vigilante violence against trans
people in the US and advice for British parents wanting to stop
LGBTQ+ lessons in schools.[29] Her 2023 rallies in Australia ran
side-by-side with Nazi marches. In London, too, fascists came
out to support her.[30] Nonetheless, Parker has managed to maintain a feminist appearance. This is actively encouraged by US
conservatives, not otherwise known for advocating for women's
rights. When Parker appeared on Tucker Carlson in 2023, she

was introduced as a 'women's rights campaigner' and 'feminist' who had been unjustly thrown out of the British left. Parker responded, 'I'm not actually a feminist... [F]eminism ringfences a movement in which all women can come together for their rights.'[31] As Bassi and LaFleur write, 'positing cis womanhood, as a putative experience, as under attack by trans people ... drafts those who would seek to protect "women" into transphobic and transmisogynist projects, and makes it easy to do so, for who is *against* protecting women?'[32] Carlson introduced Parker to his audience as if she were an English political exile who happened to find refuge in his American newsroom, set-dressed as a Disneyfied frontier homestead. He reassured Parker that the 'sex-based rights' of 'biological women' is something 'every conservative would support.' The conversation melded seamlessly with the catastrophist character of fascism. Carlson called trans rights 'civilization ending.' Parker agreed, 'it feels like the last days of Rome.'[33]

Fascism without model

Gender critical feminism is emblematic of concepts we now have to describe the accommodations of the far right by the centre. As Fran Amery and Aurelien Mondon argue, gender critical politics can be understood as a phenomenon of 'mainstreaming' in so far as 'it has been demonstrated that [gender critical] views do not represent most women ... yet this powerful pseudo-democratic argument has allowed them to gain prominence.'[34] The mainstreaming of far right discourse has become a functional part of the public sphere, and this requires persistent analysis and challenge.[35] Though far right and gender critical discourses are also artefacts of a varied historical archive that have, in the past, emerged through progressive and popular causes. Indeed, a major concern for us is that reactionary discourses are often uncritically reproduced on the left. It is not uncommon to see anti-immigration, transphobia and racism running alongside anarchist, socialist or social democratic positions. Many leftists, as we explore at the end of the book, have gone on to develop fascist associations through their transphobia. Revising our assumptions about the historical assembly of fascism can therefore help us reflect on the racial and cisnormative assembly of our own traditions and provide generative debates to challenge chauvinism and colonial nationalist themes within them.

In this book we are approaching fascism as a question that relates to race, racialisation and coloniality, and attempt to work without an ideal type, model, or previously defined criteria to contain that question. We do, however, work with the assumption that fascism and gender have a relationship to race. In this respect we consider the work of Cedric Robinson central because he relates fascism to a civilisational order that takes shape through the development of European racial projects and inventories.[36] While we agree that the interwar period is important, we also consider elemental themes of race, class, and gender within 19th century western progressive traditions as fundamental to thinking through fascism in both classical contexts and our own. And more than this we consider fascism to ultimately be a product of a long history of European racial and identity thinking, and therefore a process rather than an easily defined thing or response to things. At the fundamental level fascism is a heuristic to think about race and how racial mediation functions through cisnormative gender systems to compel political order. However, we are also mindful that fascism is a contested term and can be used to mystify liberal forms of authoritarianism that are already operational within the given political spectrum. David Renton, for this reason, cautions, 'when today the left cries fascist at people who are at a different point in the political spectrum, we waste an opportunity to challenge them.'[37] It is true that jumping to decry fascism can be stultifying, and we need theoretical models and concepts that can help us map ideological resources and alignments of the liberal democratic political spectrum rather than homogenise all reaction as fascist. Gender critical feminism in our view, however, needs to be historically related to fascism in an effort to confront how ideologically metamorphic it is.

Transmisogny is a structure of violence that is compatible

with conservative discourses of cultural decline as well as progressive defences of women's rights, which have traditionally been understood as antonyms. The threat of a boundary crossing interloper is the mobilising principle for every gender critical cadre irrespective of ideological tradition or belief. And the ease with which this figure of boundless threat synchronises with colonial myths of a racialised sexual predator and remediates antisemitic conspiracies of elites corrupting the cisnormative equilibrium of the nation – while always appearing sensible, normal, ostensibly liberal, and common sense – is perhaps unprecedented. Gender critical campaigns retain a strong affinity with the legal state that fascists traditionally sought to oppose and overturn. However, democratic lobbying and legalism, in this case, has proved able to accommodate eliminationist programmes. That neo-nazis rally to the gender critical cause does not seem to impact the respectable modulations of this movement in the same way that the Charlottesville 'Unite the Right' neo-nazi gathering impacted the respectable fronts of the so called 'alt-right' in 2017.

We should also be careful not to lose sight of the political ambivalences of 21st century fascism, even as reactionary discourses are funded, platformed and marshalled by elites. The political currencies of the contemporary gender panic – 'concerned parents', 'protecting women and children', 'mothers', 'family crisis' – do not have a straightforward conservative inheritance. They were powerful and instructive currencies of early feminist and socialist causes. As we explore in chapter one, evangelical US temperance reformers like Frances Willard campaigned on a 'home protection' platform from the 1870s to give credence to precisely these fears. Willard was understood as a conservative by many suffragists at the time, but temperance activism also had a popular basis, including in labour movements. The American second Ku Klux Klan (KKK) in the 1920s would build on these platforms in an attempt to incorporate the women's movements. It is then important not to lose sight of what is new about the far right and fascism today, but there is also a risk that even a sophisticated periodisation of the neoliberal far right will make ideological flexibility and political ambivalence a definitive mark of something new rather than an enduring feature of ideological reciprocation or relay across progressive, conservative, and fascist movement traditions over time. Traverso writes,

> Postfascism is something else: in most cases, it does indeed come from a classical fascist background, but it has now changed its forms. Many movements belonging to this constellation no longer claim such origins and clearly distinguish themselves from neofascism. In any case, they no longer exhibit an ideological continuity with classical fascism.[38]

By contrast, classical fascism is defined by Traverso as a more predictable doctrine, especially on gender issues: 'a sexist and misogynous worldview in which women would always remain submissive ... reproducers of the race; they had to take care of the home and raise children and not play a role in public life.'[39] These *were* resounding themes in 20th century fascist movements and yet active and militant women were *not* always exceptions within in the ideological leadership complexes of 'classical' fascism. Indeed, studies of women and fascism have been growing since the 1980s and 1990s as feminist historians worked to push against simple narratives of women's subservience in 'classical' fascist movements of the 1920s and 1930s. Perry Willson, the historian of Italian fascism and women, writes, 'recent studies have successfully undermined the idea that this was simply a reactionary period for women. Instead, it was full of contradictory trends, both traditional and modernizing.'[40] Willson notes how the dissolution of Italy's democratic franchise in 1925, for example, 'implied, on a purely theoretical level, some equality of the sexes since, in the new totalitarian order, no individual, of either sex, had rights. Instead, both sexes had duties to the state.'[41] As we show in chapter four, former suffragettes who joined the British Union of Fascists (BUF) saw similar possibilities. Many of the 19th and 20th century historical characters we will look at in this book moved ideological positions just as many liberal, radical,

anarchist and socialist feminists do today. These progressive figures were not bound to become fascists, but some did move that
way. Progressive families like the Pankhursts, who we look at
in chapter three, were ideologically split. Sylvia moved towards
communism and anti-colonial struggle. Christabel and Emmeline reformed the suffrage organisation as an imperialist pulpit at
the brink of war. Adela, the youngest, left Britain to help found
Australia's Communist party after World War One and by World
War Two she had joined the fascist 'Australia First' movement.

Our methodological interest in interlocking progressive and
fascist histories also presents certain risks. Ishay Landa has sought
to challenge what he calls a 'new consensus' where fascism is
'relocated ever more to the left ... if not submerging outright
into socialism, it becomes a kind of antagonistic-kindred spirit,
in many ways an analogous political force.'[42] It is true that many
liberal and conservative histories of fascism have treated socialism and fascism as kindred spirits.[43] But as the Pankhurst family
story suggests, ideological lines are rarely clear. Landa is right to
put fascism at the door of the liberal tradition. Yet he makes no
attempt to understand how 'de-massifying' tendencies emerged
from within progressive causes.[44] The historical relationship of
liberalism to fascism is conditioned by colonial and civilisational throughlines that impacted all the most radical movements.
Robinson argued that fascism could not be understood without
reassembling the civilisational trajectories of the Western project as a whole, including the labour movements and the Marxist
and progressive causes.[45] Black workers were part of Communist
Internationals in the 20th century, and they were also ostracised
by white supremacist trade unions. Feminist movements, as we
show, were just as divided. This begs the question as to how we
even come to a coherent historical identity of the 'left', never
mind how to defend it from unfair historical revisions. One way
to defend left wing history from crude horseshoe theories is to
open up moments of division within it. From this perspective, we
can release ourselves from the conventional 'pitting' or 'smudging' of ideological traditions, not only the liberal 'smudging' of

communism and fascism but also the Marxist 'pitting' of liberalism and socialism (as if the latter were not also deeply collusive with the liberal tradition).

Fascism, we accept, is a beguiling concept and overdetermined signifier. It holds such incredible power as an epistemological site of ur-evil today that few own up to being fascist. Israel shows us that European epistemologies of fascism are today providing cover for genocide.[46] The collapse of international law and the post-war liberal democratic consensus draws us back into an *ultra*-long nineteenth century, where the contradictions of that period rebound as contradictions of our own. In some ways we are closer to the movements of the 19th century, caught as they were in the deadly embrace of laissez-faire capitalism, colonialism, imperialism and racial nationalism. Western imperialism was ascendant in this era and today is in decline, but the late 19th and early 20th century progressive movements were no less obsessed by decline. Rather than seek analogies and parallels we might then ask how these movement contradictions continue to recur?

Ambivalences of progress

This book is structured in four parts and focuses largely on American and British / Irish suffrage and fascist histories. In chapter one, we look at the interlocking structures of democratic suffrage and white supremacy for 19th century women's rights struggles in the US. This includes a discussion of the progressive history of suffrage, starting at Seneca Falls. In contrast to how it is sometimes portrayed, we concentrate on what is divisive about this feminist origin story. We then look at the temperance movement, which was conservative, but developed an innovative mass movement-building apparatus. We follow this with a study of the second KKK and the Women's KKK (WKKK) in chapter two. In chapter three we look at the moral purity campaigns of Victorian middle class women. These social reformers shared an evangelical moral grammar with US temperance reformers, but their movement developed through a British imperial context.

The victimisation models those social reformers, journalists and 'purity feminists' used to campaign against prostitution are reconsidered in light of anti-trans feminist historians who claim this archive as their own. We also look at splits within the British and Irish suffragette alliance and how they were comparable to those in the US. In chapter four we study the sizeable role of women in the BUF.

The European fascist tradition is touched upon in chapter two, but no other comparative cases in interwar Europe are dealt with. There is a fascinating literature that focuses on the roles, organisations, and class compositions of women within other European cases of historical fascism.[47] Britain and the US are selected for the simple reason that they are the historical settings we know best. We first wrote this as an essay, and it turned into a book; it started as a way of bringing together our own notes with the analysis of historians, theorists and antifascist researchers working on genealogies of feminism and fascism. We also wanted to be mindful of separations that keep our fields of inquiry apart – of keeping political theory from historical specialist studies and academic writing from social movement theorising. Kathleen Blee, whose ground-breaking work on the second KKK we return to in chapter two, argues, 'scholarly guardrails can be politically debilitating, draining the political impact of our work.'[48] In her recent evaluations of gender and far right in the last decade, Blee encourages collaboration across academia, as well as political settings and spaces outside academic debate, both to understand new far right compositions and scrutinise 'the concept of a far right'.[49] Academic studies, including Blee's own, have been vital to our thinking in this book, but what academic communities can gain in analysis and terminology can also be lost on those who are thinking with liberation squarely in the forefront of their minds. In this sense we have the humbler aim of bridging specialist histories, theory, and movement conversations, for the purposes of comradely study.

Our intentions for writing this are therefore simple enough on one level but not so simple on another. This book is a record of our own conversations as we worked through movement histories and the available historical literature. These conversations have determined how we put together the history and led us to decide what histories and scenes we think are most important. We avoid theories of fascism that simply collapse in the face of historical evidence and remain sceptical of definitions that seem to exist only to be circulated. On another level, the matter is more complex, and we'll try to be as clear as we can on this before continuing. The central problem of this study is the forms of appearance fascism can take. We argue feminism has provided one such form of appearance. Fascist movements in Britain and the US were responding to the progressive era of imperialism when women dissenters and insurrectionists struggled for equal rights. Women were also being recruited into colonial formations of the family and fascist causes. Against the grain of how historical fascism is often portrayed, some feminist historians argue that women's rights causes could in fact be reconciled through fascist movements themselves. This is the specific hypothesis we've set out to explore. It's possible some may read our intentions as anti-feminist, or at least another attempt to undermine feminism, especially as so much out there does set out to achieve this. The adoption of suffragette regalia and slogans in gender critical networks, it could be argued, is mere pastiche; recuperation of a noble legacy – a perversion of *real feminism*. There is good reason to refuse the gender critical movement's feminist moniker entirely. We lean towards the argument made in *TSQ*, by other feminist critics of feminism, and feminist historians of fascism, that no authentic version of feminism exists and that its reactionary histories are as authentic to it as its most radical and internationalist contributions.

While centring historians who study women's participation in fascist movements, we do not underestimate the agency of men. On the contrary, as the Honor Oak example demonstrates, men today are able to recalibrate misogyny through transmisogyny and make it more respectable, just as male fascists of the interwar period could at times reinvent themselves and their movements through an adoption of the women's cause. It's an uneasy hypothesis to navigate. It would be disingenuous not to admit we often feel it isn't our place to explore it, but we have found encouragement from feminist comrades who consider the attempt worthwhile. In previous work on reactions to 'identity politics' and the Black feminist origins of the concept, we had similar reservations.[50] It's a risk we've come to accept because we think there's something uniquely generative about studying feminist history as a complex of ideological formations, affectivity, social reactions, colonial identity-thinking, and liberation, not as a simple vestige of progressive culture. More, as we argue, the idealisation of feminism as *good*, or indeed any labour, queer or liberation struggle as *inherently good*, is not only historically insincere, but formal to transphobic ideology which induces a classical historiography of labour traditions, gay rights and feminism against conspiracies of the 'boundary crossing' interloper. How we study reaction must therefore include a sensitivity to our own reactions to reactionary forces and the temporary shelters of certainty we make for ourselves in our concepts and our archives. In her essay 'A Feminist Politics of Ambivalence: Reading with Emma Goldman', Claire Hemmings writes, 'the uncertainty that characterises feminist and queer understandings of gender, race, and sexuality in the present is easily obscured through propositions of certainty about precisely these central concerns.'[51]

We make no claim to be experts on contemporary trans struggles either. The most we can say is that we try to listen carefully.[52] Any serious commitment to anti-fascism entails an uncomfortable crossing of lanes with the concomitant risk that we might get things wrong. We've spent a long time on the anarchist and autonomous left and seen first-hand that racial and gender literacy – that is, the critical compositional history of movements we call 'ours' – especially for men like us, is often buoyantly dismal. Anarchism, itself suffering from illusions of noble heritage, can produce proudly chauvinist anarchos, and transphobia has been a problem that is only more recently being engaged with because of the persistence of trans anarchists. Where we get things wrong, we hope to be critiqued. That isn't a matter of deference, but sensitivity to the difficulties of shared understanding and seeing across our separations. Like anyone else on the left we are compelled by the horror of the present situation. The question of division has repeatedly led the left up blind alleys of beef, grief, and conspiracy. Ugly feelings repeatedly run aground in essentialist safe harbours, which can have various expressions: zealous defences of political traditions or reductionist conceptions of race, class, and gender. Such defences often incite reactionary critiques of essentialism that are themselves essentialist. The left is itself a psychic and emotional artefact of dashed hopes, splits and betrayals that brutally compensatory correct positions hope to magic away only to further reify and reproduce. The alternative is perhaps (at risk of being miserabilist) to engage the worst of us; to study our divisions seriously, thicken out the past and our present relation to it.

1. US Suffragism and Temperance

Robert O. Paxton writes that,

> Since fascisms take their first steps in reaction to claimed failings of democracy, it is not surprising that they should appear first in the most precocious democracies, the United States and France. But we come now to a paradox: it is not necessarily in the countries that generated the first fascisms that fascist systems have had, historically, the best chance of succeeding.[1]

Paxton refers to the first Ku Klux Klan (KKK) of the post-Civil War era as one of the earliest prototypes of fascism, but argues that fascism in America failed to hurdle the 'rooting stage' that precedes the overthrow of the legal state. The first KKK emerged in reaction to the spectre of multiracial liberal democracy in the US South and quickly dissolved. The second KKK, as we show in the next chapter, was a project with no intent to overthrow the state. It developed a massive membership of women, many of whom made the transition from suffrage, temperance societies, churches and women's clubs once the right to vote was finally achieved in 1920. This fascist movement did not develop in response to democratic and economic failure, but after the successful example of the 'get out the vote' and 'do everything' campaigns of a democratic women's cause. Many white women who had been instrumental to achieving democratic suffrage rights went on to become fascist organisers within the second KKK that integrated itself within the Democratic and Republican parties.

The second KKK is a type of fascist movement that helps us to understand why George Jackson related to fascism more as an organic current within democracy than as a movement that 'takes root' before establishing itself in stages (or failing to do so).[2] As he wrote in *Blood in my Eye*: 'The warnings that "our thrusts toward self-determination will bring on fascism" are irresponsible – or better, unrealistic. The fascists already have power. The point is that some way must be found to expose them and combat them.'[3] We write this in the shadow of a genocide armed and facilitated by a Democratic Party that has demonstrated undiminished support for Israeli fascism. Progressives warned ahead of the US election that American fascism was on the horizon and Biden proved the progressive side were just as capable of shaping that horizon.

Is fascism suddenly taking on progressive appearances in America? Or has this always been the case? In the US, there has been a proportion of liberals who would put up some sort of fight against the anti-trans eliminationist and natalist reaction of the GOP. Yet many feminist Democrats have since revealed – if there were any doubts – the flexibility of the liberal feminist equal rights tradition. LGBTQ+ supporters, such as Kathy Hochul, for example, seek to replicate the 'state-wide' strategies of late suffrage by putting a comprehensive Equal Rights Amendment to the ballot in New York State, yet reacts to October 7 with support for genocide: 'If Canada someday ever attacked Buffalo, I'm sorry, my friends, there would be no Canada the next day.'[4] There are religious conservatives who ally with liberal centrist gender critical feminists and progressive liberal feminists that oppose them, but equal rights are flexibly applied and easily annulled for those excluded from a liberal progressive field enforced by colonial and imperial violence. If, following Jackson, we therefore understand fascism as an organic current within American democracy, why in this case, did it develop feminist forms of appearance? How did women leaders emerge from suffrage to defend the American racial project? Paxton is right when he says 'it is in the surrounding conditions that one must seek the differences that count, for movements that sound rather similar in their rhetoric have arrived at very different results in different national settings.'[5] The surrounding conditions we explore now are that of American suffrage and the women's cause, where we ask, how was American fascism shaped by women's questions?

We were manacled ourselves

Histories of US feminism tend not to begin with enslaved or Native women's resistance, nor proletarian migrant women's strikes in early 19th century New England, but at Seneca Falls where in 1848 the first women's rights convention was held. It was hosted by Elizabeth Cady Stanton, who like most leading lights in the movement came to women's rights through an involvement in abolitionism. Other leading figures, like Susan B. Anthony, had backgrounds in nonconformist Christianity. Yet, as abolitionism and women's suffragism grew closer to the state, leading women, unwilling to address composite framings of womanhood, became ever more abstracted from the experiences of enslaved, racialised women, domestic and factory workers – Black, immigrant and white. By 'composite' we mean a political formation of women's *causes*. There were no Black or indigenous women at Seneca Falls, nor were they mentioned. An agreed upon 'Declaration of Sentiments' was signed by attendees and published at the convention's close. This republican document repeated verbatim whole sections of Thomas Jefferson's Declaration of Independence, adding in that 'women' were also 'created equal.' It listed many of the limitations and oppressions inflicted upon women in mid-19th century America. While mentioning wages and some of the deep social and psychological harms of patriarchy in passing, more focus was given to voting, political and property rights, the legal and power constraints within marriage and the lack of rights in divorce. This was a declaration of white middle class women, addressing white ruling class men, while referring to themselves as 'one-half the people of this country.'

This was in 1848. The 1850 census shows that there were 3,204,313 enslaved people in the United States – men, women and children. There were also working class immigrant men, some of whom had few or no voting rights. Indeed, the Declaration of Sentiments uses foreign men's voting as an example of

the unfairness and humiliation faced by middle class white wom-
en: '[Man] has withheld from her rights which are given to the
most ignorant and degraded men – both natives and foreigners.'[6]
Leading Black abolitionist and former slave, Frederick Douglass,
was initially the only Seneca Falls attendee to support Stanton's
motion demanding the franchise for women. On returning
home, Douglass wrote an editorial in his *North Star* newspaper
praising the convention and underlining his support for women's
enfranchisement.[7] That same year, Douglass' daughter, Rosetta,
was first segregated then expelled from her upstate New York
school. The decision was made by a principal who was herself an
abolitionist.[8] As Black feminists and historians of suffrage have
shown, this 'first wave' universalised around the experiences of
middle class white women. Some, like Stanton, used their experience in family legal professions to envision a strategic interest
in legal sex. In turn, the legal identity of women as a class – the
aim and object of a struggle for the constitutional recognition
of women as equal – was formed by the whiteness of the movement and its class relation.

Suffragism gained momentum from the mass uprising of enslaved people and the crisis point of civil war.[9] As the possibilities for freedom expanded, alliances between social movements
were attempted. Stanton and Anthony supported Black men en-
tering the Union Army, organising a Women's Loyal League to
rally others. They toured Northern states for the Union cause,
facing hostility from pro-slavery whites and collecting 400,000
signatures to petition Congress for immediate abolition. The
American Equal Rights Association (AERA) was founded in May
1866, again by Stanton and Anthony – an attempt to combine
women's rights and abolitionist movements. Republican Party
factions pushed back, splitting this fragile alliance, favouring
only Black male suffrage in what was presented as a zero-sum
game. AERA conventions came to be dominated by rancour.
Many white delegates insisted white women were *more deserving* of suffrage than African Americans, male or female. But the
wheels were in motion to enfranchise Black men only. The re-

peated phrase was that it was 'The Negro's Hour', often justified on the basis of Black men's military service. Many white women campaigners, though certainly not all, reacted by opposing Black male suffrage. Feelings of bitterness and betrayal dominated. What began as a contingent alliance of equals, that is, Black men and middle class white women, who together envisaged something approaching universal emancipation as near and possible, became the rhetorical basis for division. Once the utopian, projective, radical equality between women and men, workers and slaves, was relinquished, an inverse, divisive equality took root, opening up a reactionary drive to reassert racial and sexual difference. How could it be that white women of high standing were now to be subservient not only to men but to *Black* men, most of whom had recently been slaves? 'Equal rights' was reframed as a backwards step for 'women' who were destined to slip down the rungs into a position on a par with or 'below' the 'Negro.' Indeed, many held to a legalistic belief that Emancipation had immediately put freed slaves on an equal footing with middle class white women.

While white women's rights leaders tended to be committed abolitionists, opposed to the ruling class of Southern slave capitalism, many had little reason to criticise Northern capitalists, some of whom were husbands, fathers, friends, supporters. Early campaigner Abby Kelley wrote: 'We have good cause to be grateful to the slave for the benefit we have received to ourselves, in working for him. In striving to strike his irons off we found most surely that we were manacled ourselves.'[10] This quote speaks to something genuine: many of the women who sparked a national movement in the 19th century *were* first politicised by their passionate involvement in anti-slavery. But in such formulations the figure of the slave was always gendered as male, while women were always white. This is a classic framework that has haunted the encounter between white and Black women's movements in America for two centuries. Stanton and Anthony, like later radical feminists, felt sexism was far more oppressive than racism or class exploitation. They saw the power wielded by men over women as *the* key oppression, made clear in the first sentence of their *History of Woman Suffrage*: 'The prolonged slavery of woman is the darkest page in human history.'[11] This framing groups together the oppression of *all* women under a unified 'slavery' during a period in which millions of women *actually experienced enslavement*, while others, including Stanton, grew up in families that *owned slaves*. From the outset, it was in the interests of wealthy white women to use such sweeping, erasive definitions of 'womanhood.' For Black women, immigrant women, working women, Native American women, queer women, or combinations of these – the picture was, and is, a lot messier. Stanton and Anthony tried to build alliances with workers but their insistence on foregrounding gendered oppression and their defence of scabbing saw them run into trouble. The history of male-dominated labour movements, and their often enthusiastic reproduction of patriarchy, is anything but proud. But Stanton's classed and racialised denigration of certain men always flowed much easier than the few times she directed criticism at the rich white men holding so much more power.

Sojourner Truth and Frances W. Harper spoke at AERA meetings about how Black women were being erased. Truth said of working women in 1867: 'I want women to have their rights. In the courts women have no right, no voice; nobody speaks for them.' Harper bravely challenged her more socially powerful white feminist counterparts. She referenced a recent assault on Harriet Tubman by a white male streetcar conductor. Harper said of Tubman:

> We have a woman in our country who has received the name of 'Moses' ... a woman who has gone down into the Egypt of slavery and brought out hundreds of our people into liberty. The last time I saw that woman, her hands were swollen. That woman who had led one of [General] Montgomery's most successful expeditions, who was brave enough and secretive enough to act as a scout for the American army, had her hands all swollen from a conflict with a brutal conductor, who undertook to eject her from her place. That wom-

an, whose courage and bravery won a recognition from our
army and from every black man in the land, is excluded from
every thoroughfare of travel.[12]

Like Harper, Tubman was a hero of the 'Underground Rail-
road,' the clandestine network of allies, safe-houses and trans-
portation for ferrying escaped slaves to Northern free states,
Mexico or Canada. Tubman made thirteen separate trips back
into slave territory. Harper demanded that delegates try to see
the world from her own vantage point and that of the great
Harriet Tubman, hero of the Combahee River Raid, abused and
dehumanised for trying to use public transport while Black. She
also protested Stanton's bourgeois construction of womanhood
in 1866. It was not as women of the bourgeois private sphere
that Harper and Tubman experienced patriarchal oppression: it
was as workers, at the hands of the law, in public space – as Black
women. There was, however, extreme resistance from bourgeois
abolitionist-suffragists to these more radical thinkers.

Disappearing horizon

Today's liberal-centrist instrumentalisation of early women's
movement history warms over the internal stresses and conflicts
that produced these splits. Consider, for example, a 2010 TED
women conference, where Nancy Pelosi recalled her first White
House visit as House minority leader. Sitting in the Oval Office,
Pelosi was suddenly crowded by the spirits of Susan B. Anthony, Elizabeth Cady Stanton and Sojourner Truth. 'I could hear
them say,' Pelosi whispered, 'at last we have a seat at the table.'[13]
Black women like Sojourner Truth or Frances W. Harper can
be summoned alongside Anthony and Stanton only as phantoms
because, in reality, their engagements with women's struggle
diverged. Both Truth and Harper supported the 15th Amendment enfranchising Black men but excluding women, and tried
to persuade white women to support it too. Historian Nell Irvin
Painter remarks mournfully how patterned this dynamic would
become:

Harper, too, rushed to defend the moral and rights of freed-
men. As black women so often have done when black men
come under attack, Harper fell silent on the rights of black
women. Concluding that she must now choose between her
identity as a woman and her identity as a Negro, she aban-
doned black women and rallied to the side of black men...
In the conflict between black men and white women, black
women disappeared.[14]

The reaction of some white women campaigners to the 15th
Amendment was incendiary. Some embarked on a turbocharged
white supremacist politics. Susan B. Anthony vowed to 'cut off
this right arm of mine before I will ever work for or demand
the ballot for the Negro and not the woman.'[15] She and Stanton moved closer to the Democratic Party, writing to its 1868
National Convention: 'While the dominant party has with one
hand lifted up two million black men and crowned them with
the honor and dignity of citizenship, with the other it has de-
throned fifteen million white women – their own mothers and
sisters, their own wives and daughters – and cast them under the
heel of the lowest orders of manhood.'[16]

The AERA fell apart upon passage of the Reconstruction
Amendments as a result of a representative split in the radical
horizon of suffrage. We call this a 'representative split' because
until this point the woman's cause was *representative of a moral
vision of equality*. As Charles Mills put it, liberalism, 'in principle at least is supposed to be committed to the nonracial moral
equality of all.'[17] This ideal could be sustained as long as suffrage
was not divided along racial and gendered lines. The movement
for suffrage was indeed divided along these lines, of course, but
the moral cause for equality helped to temper rather than ex-
acerbate those divisions. The opposition of 'woman' to 'Negro'
in the 15th amendment not only marked a divide in the idea
of universal suffrage down the colour line, and the end of the
abolitionist gesture in the women's movement, it erased Black
and indigenous women from the struggle entirely. This 'white
blindspot' (or intentional erasure) has been a persistent feature

of every feminist 'wave' since.

Debates around the rights and wrongs of episodes in feminist history are therefore important because they are complex and wrought. Historians of suffrage can help to challenge essentialism in our movements because it is clear that womanhood had no stable identity. Indeed, the role of state power in splitting movement alliances becomes far clearer when an idealised story of national women's rights struggle is troubled. Historian Ellen Carol Dubois is right to reflect on how radical many aspects of the early women's movement were. With Stanton and Anthony as two of its leading lights, the movement fought tirelessly against sexism in society. Dubois shows their ideas changing and developing over the course of their long lives:

> From one perspective, suffragism in the years immediately following the Civil War was a very radical movement. Its leaders – especially Elizabeth Cady Stanton and Susan B. Anthony – cooperated with Victoria Woodhull and William Sylvis, free love advocates, the labor movement and even with the First International. In order to understand the nature of woman's oppression and the possibility of her emancipation, suffragists found themselves drawn more and more toward the most advanced aspects of nineteenth-century political thought. They identified and criticized capitalism as a major source of woman's oppression, addressed themselves to the position of working women, spoke out boldly against the sexual double standard and exploitation of women, and were beginning to identify marriage and the family – even more than political disfranchisement – as the basic source of woman's oppression. Such a politics deserves to be called radical, because of both the breadth to which it aspired and the particular positions it took.[18]

It was also, however, a consistently racist politics and one that had a particular class character from which it wouldn't or couldn't escape – or perhaps even recognise. The movement failed to encompass a capacious enough breadth of composition to organise 'womanhood.' Its demands were less of a priority, its modes of organisation less accessible, to most women in America. The collapse of the AERA signified a disappearing horizon for a shared struggle for women's rights and Black liberation. The representative split that segregated a common emancipatory movement for equal rights by 'sex' led then to a movement split. The women's cause was acrimoniously split off into two separate organisations. The American Woman Suffrage Association maintained a mixed male and female leadership and membership, it foregrounded Black male suffrage as a priority and was committed to staying tied to the Republican Party's reform wing in hopes that eventually it would prioritise a woman suffrage amendment. Radical Republicanism's reforming zeal died, however, with Reconstruction and it never delivered on its promises. The National Woman Suffrage Association marked the break up of abolitionism and feminism under the leadership of Stanton and Anthony. This female-led organisation prized women's self-activity and autonomy in its pursuit of a wider vision of emancipation – not only the franchise but a more transformative, revolutionary change to women's roles within the household and wider society. To achieve their goal, Stanton and Anthony bitterly rejected the Republican Abolitionist reform coalition they had been at the heart of for two decades, casting their net wide for new alliances. This included openly white supremacist Democratic politicians and financing to match their increasingly racist arguments for white women's rights, early labour unions who they ultimately couldn't find common ground with and a rising cohort of middle class, independent white women, particularly in Midwest states, as its new social base.

A divisive equality

These strands eventually reunited in 1890 to create the National American Woman Suffrage Association (NAWSA). This organisation publicly supported, and reproduced in its structures, the worsening conditions of African Americans. It adopted policies demanding literacy requirements for voting, explicitly seeking to ensure the ongoing disenfranchisement of Black women. At the 1901 NAWSA convention in Minneapolis, an octogenarian Susan B. Anthony announced that through women's 'intelligent emancipation [the white race] will be purified... [I]t is through woman [that] the race is to be redeemed.'[19] Replacing Anthony as NAWSA president was Carrie Chapman Catt. In her conference address, Catt outlined three main obstacles standing in the way of women's equality: militarism, responsible for making politics seem a masculine pursuit; prostitution, for giving women a bad name; and 'inertia' about the expansion of American democracy which, according to her, 'with possibly ill-advised haste, enfranchised the foreigner, the negro, and the Indian. Perilous conditions, seeming to follow from the introduction into the body politic of vast numbers of irresponsible citizens, have made the nation timid.'[20] At the 1903 NAWSA convention, held in New Orleans, one delegate warned that Southern Black people were being allowed to educate themselves and that this would lead to 'race war.' Belle Kearney of Mississippi worried that 'the poor white man, embittered by his poverty and humiliated by his inferiority, finds no place for himself and his children, then will come the grapple between the races.'[21] Kearney saw the solution to preventing this 'unspeakable culmination,' not in civil and equal rights for all, nor the abolition of the social conditions that produced both 'poverty' and 'inferiority' but instead suggested that, 'the enfranchisement of women will have to be effected, and an educational and property qualification for the ballot be made to apply. The enfranchisement of [white] women would insure immediate and durable white supremacy, honestly attained.'[22] Kearney here, perhaps more explicitly but not out of step with her movement, presented the enfranchisement of privileged white women as an effective bulwark for maintaining white supremacy.

The reunified women's suffrage movement also came to embrace an expanding imperialism, buoyed by turn of the century US invasions of Cuba, the Philippines, Hawaii, Guam and Puerto Rico. US imperialism was underpinned by an ideology of moral and racial improvement that 'exceptional' America would bring to 'savage' populations. Women's suffrage had emerged during a time of national conflict and national rebuilding, and was couched in the language of national citizenship and constitutional rights. But it developed through an age of imperialist expansion. Suffragists had to decide how to orient themselves to this new political terrain. Allison Sneider argues that 'the history of the U.S. woman suffrage movement is also inseparable from the history of U.S. expansion and the related political rights for potential new citizens that expansion inevitably raised.' Sneider explains that the ideological concepts, discourses and limits of the movement are bound up with their relationship to imperialism:

> By the end of the nineteenth century, many suffragists were increasingly well versed in the language of empire. In this imperial frame of reference, voting was less a right of citizenship than of civilization, and less defined by universal inclusion than by a shared capacity to exercise the privileges of democracy based on a combination of racial traits and religious commitments.[23]

It is a significant departure to see how, within a generation, suffragist visions for a more inclusive, though nonetheless settler-colonial, republic began to transition towards the ideals of an empire, expanding conceptually to divide the world up between the civilised and the not.

As Ellen Carol Dubois states, the paths taken by America's early women's suffrage leaders are hard to disconnect from their social backgrounds: '[they] were rarely from the ranks of wage-earners. Some, like [Lucy] Stone and Anthony, were the daughters of small farmers. Others, most notably Stanton, were the children of considerable wealth.'[24] After the word 'male' entered into the Constitution for the first time, Stanton wrote in 1866: 'if that word "male" be inserted, it will take us a century at least to get it out.' In fact, once Reconstruction was overthrown and white supremacy reasserted, it was a century before Black Americans finally had *some* civil rights enforced by the federal government. Meanwhile, white women secured voting rights with the 20th Amendment in 1920. For Stanton and Anthony, the betrayal of 'womanhood' by Black male suffrage could only be reduced to a conspiracy of male supremacy, Black and white. The lesson Stanton took: woman 'must not put her trust in man.'[25] While shared patriarchy was an element, Black male enfranchisement came about in large part due to Republican Party strategy and the Northern bourgeoisie's attempt to secure post-war Reconstruction. That is, a calculation was made: Black men would vote Republican, enfranchised white women would return the white supremacist Democrats to power.[26]

A major fracture in the US suffrage movement was the introduction of sex-based rights into the constitution, because it would mean women were legally segregated. The women were against it. In this way, at least, gender critical campaigns to put 'biological women' into state and federal law suggests a reaction against the historical cause of feminism. Firstly, because gender critical feminism mobilises the patriarchal state against the prospective ideal of moral equality. It functions to destroy the rights that have been fought for on that basis. Secondly, this movement takes the perspective of the patriarchal state to enforce a *divisive, cisnormative equality* and seeks to achieve this by scanning for and inciting rifts in contemporary emancipatory currents. To this effect, 'real women' are opposed to trans women – and therein authenticated as real – through state violence. The 'LGB' is rescued from 'the T' through state violence. 'Children' become opposed to 'Transgender children' through state violence. It is not difficult to imagine how excited evangelical conservatives must have been to realise that a whole menu of rights-destroying schemes could be activated through the progressive appearance of the gender critical movement. Yet it is also too comforting to think of such progressive appearances as masks – a trojan horse for conservative anti-feminism. Progressive movements for moral equality and eugenic and racial notions of sex difference developed conterminously through every section of the 19th century and 20th century women's cause. Many of the most progressive sections had this ambivalent structure.

The new womanhood

Winnifred Harper Cooley was a cadre of Carrie Chapman Catt and NAWSA, who represented a more metropolitan and forward thinking feminism on one level. Her writings evidence a desire to escape the trappings of sex as an established fact in and of itself. As she wrote, 'If the keynote of the present uprising of womanhood were to be sounded, it would be "No sex in brain, in mind or morals!"'[27] Cooley was of a generation concerned with the productive place of women in the new industrial setting and disdainful of a woman's sphere removed from questions of labour, technological advance and modern civic society. Indeed, what womanhood could become was an idiom of experimentation for new generations of Progressive Era women anticipating a sea change in gender relations. In 1913, Cooley registered this shift by referring to herself, specifically, as a feminist, 'we have grown accustomed ... to something or other known as the Woman Movement. That has an old sound – it is old. But Feminism!' Jane Mansbridge writes that 'by 1913, Feminism with a capital F had been embraced by the more radical women in the movement. The goal for them, as distinct from mere suffrage, was, as one young woman put it, "a complete social revolution," in which women could express themselves freely.'[28] The term feminism had a reasonably short lifespan in the Progressive Era and Cooley is one of few Anglophone figures to be cited using it before it was revived in the 1960s.[29]

Cooley's feminism was non-clerical and averse to traditional notions of womanhood, but her break with the 'old sound' was used to establish a new sound that took the progressive inheritance and used it to prospect a proto-fascist, femo-nationalist vision. What we might term 'proto-fascist feminism' proper is apparent as early as 1904 in Cooley's 'New Womanhood' essay. It begins from a progressive vision, which Cooley establishes through the rise of the woman's club:

The growth of America's clubs since 1852 has been phe-
nomenal. Every village has its attempt at a club, more or less
imposing, while every city swarms with societies, in which
the same women are apt to duplicate and reduplicate their
membership. The National Federation has nearly 4,000 clubs,
including a membership of 220,000... Besides the federation
of literary clubs, there is the National Council of Women,
the broadest conception thus far embodied, as its scope is
nothing less than the union of all National bodies of women,
of which there are in this country about *one hundred*. Already
the National Council comprises twenty-four organizations,
each of which is National (such as the Woman's Christian
Temperance Union)... The Council of the United States
numbers over 1,000,000 women. There are now twenty-three
countries that have National Councils of Women modeled
upon our own (Great Britain, France, Italy, Sweden, etc.) and
all of these, in 1898, at the instigation of an American woman, united to form an *International* Council of Women, which
is larger and more comprehensive in its scope than any body
of men, with *diversified* interests, in the world.[30]

Cooley had international ambitions for this movement and yet
this transition into the new would be modelled on ancient runes
and traditional maxims. The modern 'woman's club' is traced
back to ancient Greece: 'on the sunny Isle of Lesbos, Sappho
founded the first *woman's club*, and wrote immortal lyrics, 600
years before Christ!'[31] The prolific creativity of what Cooley refers to as the old woman becomes a residual inspiration for what
the new woman might achieve in the new century. Cooley then
offers an economically minded vision of a society of free individuals and free labour, within Malthusian proportions: 'The real
solution is not ... in the over-stocking of the market, but it is the
training of the illiterate and low-born (possibly the compulsion
of the diseased and criminal) to cease from undesirable reproduction!'[32] The woman's club could be the organisational unit to
advance this eugenicist program:

The woman's club will be in the broadest sense a civic club, because civic life is only less vital than home life, which is its foundation. City government is only housekeeping upon a large scale. *Economy*, from the Greek, means 'law of the house,' and political economy is the law of the household carried into the community. Women have the training of the ages back of them in domestic economics; what class is better fitted to undertake the problems of our cities?[33]

The traditional maxim, 'Home is where the heart is', was Cooley's favoured expression and she sought to give it a modern meaning by rethinking *oikos* for the new age. As Angela Mitropoulos explains,

In the oikonomic schema it is sexuality and gender difference that reproduces the purportedly unique properties of the *oikos*, and race is the exemplary motif of a unique and heritable property. Concepts of race always hinge on concepts of a heteronormative sexuality and genealogy, since it is ostensibly through sex that race is reproduced.[34]

1904 was nearly a half century on from the 'Negro's hour' and the AERA splits, yet Cooley still asks, regretfully, 'why did our country enter into a heartrending war to free a race of illiterate black people, making the final issue, the giving of these black men the citizen's badge of honor, the ballot; yet totally ignore the intelligent, moral white women in every home, utterly deprived of political power.'[35] The 'Negro's hour' represented a betrayal of the *oikos* for Cooley, and the 'new womanhood' a vision to restore it.

As we are applying the term 'proto-fascist feminism' to Cooley, we may pause to ask how this term is adequate. Cooley is not so far from the white supremacism of Stanton and Anthony, so why is her feminism proto-fascist and theirs not? The desire to pedagogically shape the masses 'so that they shall cease to be masses' is a criterion for fascism advanced by Landa and a useful one, except that progressive reform movements were often or-

ganising to do just this.[36] Stanton and Antony's turn to a more
full-throated white supremacism came with a wish to quell the
Black masses. Cooley's femo-nationalism includes a vision to nationalise the masses based on racialised eugenic principles. David
Renton argues, 'at its heart, fascism is reactionary; it desires to
advance capitalist technology while restoring society to the class
peace it wrongly associates with the years prior to 1789.'[37] As a
result of the dissolution of the women's cause, Cooley reconstructs a mythic relationship to time and embraces technological
development. Perhaps this combination of factors sets Cooley
apart from her predecessors, in particular her vision for a total
industrial reorganisation of society spearheaded by elite women
and their bourgeois male equals. 'The problem of propagation
is being solved by the thinking few,' she wrote, 'by a process of
elimination.'[38] *Proto*-fascist feminist, too, because Cooley did not
organise a fascist cause, or form a fascist practice, to substantiate
this hypothesis. Yet the specific development of the US racial regime may complicate our terms since Cooley saw this process of
elimination already developing through the civil infrastructures
of this young democracy. Her actionism of the *oikos* and call to
take the law of the household into the city was, from her perspective,
already underway.

Home protection!

If fascism is indeed related to a reassertion of the *oikos* – an ontol-
ogy of household order that seeks to redefine equality through a
contract between those deemed to share in the racial inheritance
– we can hardly think of fascism without also thinking through
early feminist theories of the family and the nation. Mitropou-
lous writes that the 'brutal father-fuhrer is pivotal to fascism's
conflation between nation and family.'[39] Early feminist currents
prototyped this conflation in various ways. Progressives sought
to expand the law of the household to the civic functions of the
liberal administrative state and provided a national vision for
womanhood on this step. Stanton and Anthony withdrew from
the cause of moral equality to pursue the vote for white women

like themselves. Cooley, however, was envisioning an instrumental reshaping of political economy via the law of the household. Indeed, part of her eugenic vision for women was a broader vision for labour equality,

> In the sweet reason of our larger day, Each must his work contribute to the whole, Knowing, together, we must rise or fall. Man will not look to God, and woman find 'Her God in Man,' as sang the bigot-bard, But both will pray and toil in unison, Finding the sweetness of togetherness, United labor, heaven upon earth![40]

Cooley's utopia resounds through the erasure of those we know to be excluded from 'the new paradise' – the 'illiterate Black men', 'diseased', 'criminal'. As Melinda Cooper argues, 'family responsibility served as a rallying cry for classical liberals and moral conservatives alike … [and] enabled the peculiar alliance between radical free-market economics and moral traditionalism that flourished in late nineteenth-century America.'[41] Indeed, differentiating conservative drafts of family responsibility, from progressive visions for the family, is not so easy. The family and the nation were points of articulation between various and seemingly incompatible sections of the suffrage cause.

It is useful to compare, for example, Cooley's metropolitan branch of NAWSA proto-fascist feminism, which emerges through the Northern suffrage tradition, to the most successful federation of women's clubs of the period, the Women's Christian Temperance Union (WCTU), which served to organise more religiously conservative communities. Male-led temperance movements were nascent from the 1820s, before a Women's Temperance Crusade in 1873-74 brought many more women into the fold. The WCTU was set up in 1874 to institutionalise the temperance crusades against alcohol, before it expanded to include the women's ballot. Historians of temperance have debated the exact relationship this movement had to the early feminist figures of suffrage and many key figures, as we shall see, were wary of it.[42] However, Richard H. Chused argues convincingly that temperance gave fuel to the women's cause:

> Suffrage and temperance arose from similar instincts, each
> spurred by an increasing recognition of the roles of wom-
> en in American society and their importance in shaping the
> nature of national political culture. And both temperance
> and suffrage took the leap from state control – in both cases
> adopting ideas already accepted in many states – to national
> standards.[43]

By 1892, the WCTU had 200,000 dues-paying members, while
NAWSA had only 13,000.[44] This popularity was partly due to a
recruitment style and organisational strategy suited to the more
cautious temper of conservative and evangelical communities.
Unlike the suffragist appeal to reason, typically heard by sympathetic liberal audiences, or Cooley's feminist lyric to civic pro-
ductivism, WCTU leader Frances Willard oriented the woman's
question around threats to the traditional family home. The title
of her most famous speech, 'Home Protection', as Suzanne M.
Marilley notes, was 'shorthand rationale for tariff policy' and
part of the lexicon of economic protectionism at the time.[45] Willard used this nativist metaphor for economic security to associate the disintegrative effects of alcohol with a moral cataclysm
of home and nation: 'God has indicated woman, who is the born
conservator of home, to be the Nemesis of home's arch enemy,
King Alcohol.'[46] In effect women were called upon to *reapply the
oikonomic schema to contaminations of the home* and to rescue the
father from resorting to domestic violence. Willard believed that
mothers and daughters were put on Earth to conserve a moral
equilibrium, something men, prone to vice and drink, were ill
equipped to do. It was women, the purer sex, Willard argued,
who would have to take this fight to the ballot box: 'in a republic,
this power of hers may be most effectively exercised by giving
her a voice in the decision by which the rum-shop door shall
be opened or closed beside her home.'[47] Through biblical mandate, Willard believed women could be inspired to challenge
patriarchs who had fallen for drink and vice, because no man

was ultimately higher than God. Women would then join the movement for suffrage and emancipate society as a whole from cultural decline. Importantly, women were invited to participate in this movement *as mothers*. As Marilley argues, 'other notable women used motherhood to develop ideologies, but Willard is the only one who used it to mobilize mass numbers of women to undermine male domination.'[48] Willard achieved unprecedented recruitment, especially within communities where traditional gender relations were seemingly unshakeable, 'including membership in its juvenile societies, the WCTU grew under Willard's leadership in the 1880s from 27,000 to nearly 200,000.'[49]

Marilley has called temperance activism the 'feminism of fear' and it was arguably the most popular American feminism of the 19th century, due to the breadth of issues the movement evolved to confront and the populist traditions it crossed over with.[50] The WCTU could also be incredibly militant and was more concretely aligned with labour than most suffragist organisations. The Knights of Labor, which had many women workers in its ranks, brought temperance teachings to bear on issues of internal conduct between workers. 'Lady Knights' benefited from formal gender equality within the membership and a conception of labour that was more expansive and gender inclusive than in many other nascent labour unions. Housewives and wage earning women were invited to join with equal privileges. Women and babies were welcome at local assemblies to 'tone up the meeting' and contributed to a reform of the assembly format, which traditionally took place in the saloon.[51] The Knights and temperance unions were remarkably inclusive for the time, organising across gender lines, and occasionally across colour and religious lines. Though as Susan Levine writes, 'lady Knights did not challenge the notion of a domestic sphere for women. Rather, like many nineteenth-century feminists, they believed in a particularly feminine sensibility, one that upheld the values of hearth and home and that could at the same time infuse the public world with a more moral, humane, and cooperative character.'[52] Yet at the same time, WCTUs would occupy saloons,

pharmacies and breweries and shut them down. Suffrage campaigners were sometimes aghast at such direct action religiosity.
A letter from Miriam Cole reads,

> A woman knocking out the head of a whiskey barrel with an
> ax, to the tune of Old Hundred, is not the ideal woman sit-
> ting on a sofa, dining on strawberries and cream, and sweetly
> warbling, 'The Rose that All are Praising.' She is as far from
> it as Susan B. Anthony was when pushing her ballot into the
> box. And all the difference between the musical saint spilling
> the precious liquid and the unmusical saint offering her vote
> is, that the latter tried to kill several birds with one stone, and
> the former aims at only one.[53]

Stanton criticised the temperance crusades as 'mob law' and others continued to criticise the particularism of an issue-based campaign.[54] However, under Willard, it soon expanded to encompass
a 'do everything' philosophy, including campaigns against child
labour, trafficking, an eight hour day, and the vote for women.
The fight against vice, alcohol and moral decay could also become a rationale for affixing weak moral reasoning to lesser and
inferior 'races.' In Willard's last WCTU national convention address in 1893, she called on Congress to 'enact a stringent immigration law prohibiting the influx into our land of more of the
scum of the Old World, until we have educated those who are
here.'[55] As late as the 1890s, Willard publicly advocated 'Colonization' – that is, the wholesale repatriation of African Americans
to West Africa or Haiti, as a solution to the 'Negro Problem.'[56]
She suggested such a scheme was in the interests of all: 'If I
were black and young, no steamer could revolve its wheels fast
enough to convey me to the dark continent. I should go where
my color was the correct thing, and leave these pale faces to
work out their own destiny.' Willard also connected sexual violence to Black masculinity, as Stanton and Anthony had before
her. Amid the nadir of lynching violence in the South, Willard
claimed Black men were more prone to alcohol abuse and, therefore, more prone to sexual violence. In the early postbellum peri-

od, lynching against African Americans had mostly been justified as a defence against Black revolt. This justification lost narrative salience with the overthrow of Reconstruction and the solidification of Jim Crow rule. It was replaced by a narrative of lynching as a form of righteous vengeance against the constructed moral panic figure of the 'Black rapist.' This myth was believed and perpetuated by a cross section of white society, North and South, and persists as a thoroughly colonial feature of racist discourse up to this day. Black women led the campaign against lynching nationwide (and across the Atlantic, as campaigners also raised awareness and agitated in Britain).[57] Journalist Ida B. Wells had driven the movement since 1892, when her friend was murdered in Memphis and she was forced to flee the South. As the practice persisted, campaigners tried to get white women involved but the full weight of the white women's movement did not support their efforts. Wells publicly criticised Willard as an 'apologist for lynching' as did others in the anti-lynching cause.[58] Black women within the WCTU, such as Lucy Thurman, who would go on to be president of the National Association of Colored Women (NACW), refrained from criticism and were 'caught in the cross-fire.'[59]

In a recent, fascinating doctoral study of race, immigration and politics within the WCTU, Ella Wagner assesses the tensions that the racial nexus of the period produced in the organisation.[60] Thurman, as Wagner discusses, had been a persistent critic of a 'colour line' functioning within the WCTU institutions and yet she continued to work within them even 'as the prohibition movement overall turned more firmly to racist arguments and tactics.'[61] Wagner points to the ambivalences of this period. Despite the intervention from Ida B. Wells, 'Black women actually joined [the WCTU] in even greater numbers in the subsequent years.'[62] At the same time, the organisation became even more segregated by race and by tactics. Black temperance activists began to work more autonomously under the umbrella of prohibition as 'white women increasingly defined their prohibition and anti-rape activism in terms of controlling the imagined threat of violent, drunken Black men and preserving the "purity" of the white race.' 'Meanwhile,' Wagner writes. 'Black women made greater use of the rhetoric of "protection" and aimed their efforts at the systems – liquor traffic, incarceration, sexual violence, and racist terror – that threatened Black people in general and Black women in particular.'[63] It wasn't until 1930 that an Association of Southern Women for the Prevention of Lynching was founded. These white women did bravely campaign in the face of threats and intimidation, collecting thousands of signatures for their pledge demanding the 'eradicat[ion] [of] lynchings and mobs forever from our land.'[64] But it was too little too late. As Mary Church Terrell, co-founder of the NACW, said in 1904, 'What a mighty foe to mob violence Southern white women might be, if they would arise in the purity and power of their womanhood to implore their fathers, husbands and sons no longer to stain their hands with the black man's blood!'[65] Wagner notes a reassertion of whiteness within the temperance movement as well: 'In 1919, only four Black state unions – in DC, Maryland, Florida, and South Carolina – remained, down from twelve just two years earlier. By 1923, the WCTU had renamed the department of Colored Work to "Work Among Negroes." A white superintendent from Georgia, Mamie Emma Wood Williams, led it.'[66] This segregationist tendency within the union converged with a fraternal organisational network that drew recruits and experience from its white supremacist ranks.

2. The Women of the Ku Klux Klan

My nature is serious, righteous and just,
And tempered with the love of Christ.
My purpose is noble, far-reaching and age-lasting.
My heart is heavy, but not relenting;
Sorrowful but not hopeless;
Pure but ever able to master the unclean;
Humble but not cowardly;
Strong but not arrogant;
Simple but not foolish;
Ready, without fear.
I am the Spirit of Righteousness.
They call me the Ku Klux Klan.
I am more than uncouth robe and hood
With which I am clothed.
YEA, I AM THE SOUL OF AMERICA

Daisy Douglass Barr, leader of Indiana's Women's KKK
(1923)[1]

The first iteration of the KKK in the 1860s used racist terror to help overthrow Reconstruction. Half a century later the second Klan made the same bet the Republican bourgeoisie did in our last chapter: once white women got the vote, this could provide a boon to white supremacy. Launched in 1915 in Georgia by William Joseph Simmons, the second Klan had initially fed off the success of the movie *Birth of a Nation*, which was screened only weeks after the lynching of a Jewish man, Leo Frank, in Marietta, Georgia, after he was convicted of murdering a white girl.[2] The organisation grew slowly at first, largely confined to a male membership of 5-6,000 Klan revivalists in Georgia and Alabama, until Mary Elizabeth Tyler and Edward Clarke, colleagues at an Atlanta public relations firm, got involved, applying modern business acumen to the flailing organisation.[3] The first Klan was overwhelmingly known for its anti-Black violence and its mission to maintain Southern white supremacy despite the defeat of the Confederacy. While the 1920s Klan's anti-Black focus was undiminished, Tyler and Clarke helped broaden its emphasis to new 'threats' – immigrants, Catholics, Jews, Communists – that could be emphasised more or less depending on the locality. Tyler also set up a women's auxiliary to the organisation, the Women's KKK (WKKK). Membership of the second KKK subsequently exploded between 1921-1924, during a period of rapid change. Black and working class militancy intensified after World War One and immigration increased as US colonial and industrial expansion required ever more settlers and labour. Black migration to Northern states was met with violent racism and the spectre of communism frightened the propertied classes (large and small). For the Klan, communism was invariably coded as Jewish conspiracy and portended the downfall of monogamy and racial hierarchy – the ideological and material basis of America.

Histories of the second Ku Klux Klan present a certain incongruence with how we expect fascist movements to take root. While the anti-socialist and anti-IWW currents of the American progressive era were certainly central to its development, it is more difficult to understand this model of American fascism as a reaction to democracy. That women had powerful roles within the organisation was reflective of the mass education of women through civic institutions, church groups and clubs. The Woman's Christian Temperance Union, as we explored in the last chapter, was instrumental to this. This women's organisation presented a rupture with traditional forms of patriarchal subordination, as rural, working class and middle class women became agents of democratic mobilisation and even some Black women members could draw from philosophies of Christian sisterhood. Yet temperance was centrally motivated by moral conservation and mitigating racial and civilisational decline by biblical mandate and ballot. Temperance can, in this way, be understood as one important gateway into the WKKK, not only because many temperance organisers, and suffragists, joined the Klan, bringing immense organising experience to the cause, or because the moral cadence of the polemics were often similar, but because the natalist synthesis of home and nation in the temperance movement had been so instructive as a successful organising model of movement growth.

Feminist historians of the WKKK, whose work inspires the investigation of this chapter, have done important work to shine a light on the connections between suffrage and temperance activism and this early 20th century fascist formation. Nancy MacLean writes how 'the Klan even adopted a take-off on the female temperance motto, 'For God, Home and Native Land.'[4] Willard's 1879 'Home Protection Manual' offered a breakthrough organising model that invited women to focus on the home, community and civic institutions as the means to change the state of the nation. This manual combined arresting rhetoric with empirical instruction on how to build social reform platforms.[5] The WCTU continued to develop alongside the WKKK, and experienced organisers created recruitment relays between organisations. *Twenty lessons on government, ten lessons in Indiana government,* published in 1919, offers a glimpse into the evolution of temperance publishing culture at the threshold of the WKKK's emergence.[6] The manual provides a detailed analysis of Indiana state law and its relationship to federal law, introduced thus: '[T]hese short lessons in government are prepared not only for study and discussion in the bi-monthly meetings of the Unions, but also for use at home with the members of the family.'[7] The restrictionist flourishes that organised the temperance rhetorical tradition since the 19th century are interspersed with legal information and civic directories of every decision maker in the state:

A great question is facing the nation. Will the third generation be American? It is not necessary to learn or to try to learn immigration facts and figures. If women use eyes and ears, they must see over stores, in newspapers, even in lists of city government officials many foreign names; and they cannot but hear on the streets, trains and trollies and in the stores foreign tongues. And the children everywhere![8]

In a collection of interviews with ex-members of the Indiana WKKK undertaken in the 1980s, Kathleen Blee emphasises the degree of innocence and community mindedness that these women projected back to their movement,

Store owners, teachers, farmers ... the good people all belonged to the Klan... They were going to clean up the government, and they were going to improve the school books [that] were loaded with Catholicism. The pope was dictating what was being taught to the children, and therefore they were being impressed with the wrong things.[9]

An Indiana native living in Arkansas, Lulu Markwell, was the first Imperial Commander of the WKKK and under her leadership, Blee notes,

Female field agents and kleagles ... worked with KKK kleagles to bring the message of the women's Klan to all areas of the country... [F]emale nativist and patriotic societies, in particular, were courted by WKKK organizers who sought to persuade them to merge into the new national women's Klan.[10]

Markwell had been the long-serving President of the Arkansas WCTU as well as a leading local suffragist and, along with her husband, an influential member of Arkansas' Democratic Party. Markwell noted that 'women's interest in politics, once latent, had been piqued by the Nineteenth Amendment granting women the vote.'[11] Women now saw it as their duty to work 'in the maintenance of that amendment.'[12] Daisy Douglas Barr, leader of Indiana's WKKK, had also headed up a women's club, the Queens of the Golden Mask, before it was absorbed into the Klan. She was an evangelist Quaker preacher from the age of 16 and a WCTU member, known locally as a rousing speaker.

Barr often travelled with male Klan leaders on national speaking tours, proving to be a powerful recruitment asset: 'Barr was very successful in organizing women for temperance, attracting sixteen hundred women to a single meeting. Children sang her name at temperance anti-liquor events, "Easy Daisy, Who's a Daisy, Daisy Douglas Barr."'[13] Like many women in the WKKK, Barr had a politically ambivalent past. A critic of church members who used racial slurs, the sexual double standard and advocate of women's members for the church in the 1910s, Barr was elected president of American War Mothers in 1920, before being chucked out in 1923 as being a Klan leader threatened the reputation of the organisation.[14]

Incredible growth of the membership meant that for a while, the KKK grew into a multimillion pound enterprise. What we term 'commercial fascism' seemed to buck the 20th century trend, since this form of fascism emerged within a highly developed administrative state and integrated into democratic civic society, rather than vowing to replace it. Italian fascism emerged in the same period and managed to dissolve the democratic state. The KKK, by contrast, seemed to go up like a skyscraper before dissolving without a trace. Yet the hypothesis we explore here is that the second KKK is perhaps even more relevant to how we understand fascist mobilisation today because a highly developed and resilient democratic infrastructure offered members extraordinary organising opportunities to exploit the proceeds of racial capitalism without 'overturning' democracy. Even though the second KKK imposed a religious restriction on white supremacy it was otherwise able to build fascist pluralities through local power brokers (churches, labour men, cops, businesses) and the political expertise of women drawn from suffrage activism, temperance organisations and preaching circuits. Regional cross-class compositions were reflected in the membership lists along with *the mass participation of women*. Indeed, the fraternal quality of the organisation would perhaps only be suggestive of a particular stage of economic development except for the fact that this American model of fascist activism and enterprise culture has come to define the gender critical and evangelical networks of the social media age. These 'family orientated' strategies were revived by conservative women's activists in the New Right or New Christian Right in the 1980s, 1990s and again in the 2010s, where, as Kathleen Blee writes, 'small groups of women assembling to write letters to politicians … created a model of "kitchen table activism."'[15] Indeed, the 'gender resource guides' produced by contemporary anti-trans lobbying groups, such as Moms for Liberty, show how the women's club and the distribution of 'home protection manuals' remain critical to 21st century fascist formation.[16]

Mothers of the race

The WKKK was set up in June 1923 and 'by November … chapters existed in 36 states, claiming 250,000 members age 16 and older.'[17] At its height, it boasted half a million nationwide.[18] The Klan's male leadership became open to women members partly for financial reasons, not wanting to close off half their potential market. There had been pressure too from white women already involved in white supremacist women's groups, wanting to join the Klan. As Blee writes:

> The WKKK absorbed many women's secret societies and nativistic leagues, including the … League of Protestant Women, Ladies of the Cu Clux Clan, Ladies of the Golden Mask, Order of American Women, Ladies of the Golden Den, Hooded Ladies of the Mystic Den, and Puritan Daughters of America.[19]

The Klan's need to compete with organisations already growing in popularity contributed to their decision to open up membership to white Protestant women. Internal competition within the KKK also played its part. As different factions of Klansmen vied for the national leadership, they could see the benefit of broadening their support base by building good relations with WKKK members. The new reality of women's suffrage was a game changer. With electoral politics a key terrain for the new Klan, the dismissal of women as political actors would have gone against their interests. The Klan needed white, '100% American' women's suffrage for their project. Indeed – as with Stanton and Anthony – race, ethnicity and religion were once again mobilised to argue for white Protestant women's rights *in particular* and *in competition* with those of anyone who wasn't '100% American.' The Klan insisted that it was the best guarantor of white Protestant women's rights, that they alone 'could safeguard women's suffrage and expand women's other legal rights while working to preserve white Protestant supremacy.'[20]

Women who took leadership roles in the KKK did so after becoming relatively high profile campaigners, preachers or lecturers within women's clubs and suffrage organisations. Already in 1904, Winnifred Harper Cooley, whose 'new womanhood' we looked at in the last chapter, spotted something in the progressive era transition that had alerted her to a vital new potential for women, but a worrying trend for men: 'intellectuality among men is decreasing, among women, increasing. Already, it is the condition in the average family that the wife attends lectures, concerts, clubs, reads magazines and books, while the husband is chained to business interests.'[21] The women had run on a cause that, in truth, held together a range of ideological interests, but the more total trend, Cooley believed, was that women had gained an intellectual steer on the men:

> We are living in a period of transition. Business women are pioneers with the eyes of the world upon them. With them rests the freedom of future women. Their conduct does not need to be merely as frank and open and decent as that of the average business man, but must be exemplary. They must be all tact, discretion, must use a nice sense of discrimination – there must be no obtrusion of sex in business, yet no bold loss of it. In short, they must possess the diplomacy of the French salon, but must banish its coquetry. The woman in business must possess camaraderie without coarseness, self-reliance without self-consciousness, wholesome morals,

firm principles, and good sense.[22]

Cooley had a vision for a complementary feminism of the American private family enterprise, 'to be two in unity, is better than to be one!'[23] – a motto exemplified by the power couples of the Klan. What we see here is a convergence of progressive and conservative archetypes one might typically consider separate: the rights-based feminist, the corporate feminist and the evangelical conservative. Daisy Douglas Barr went on to become the first female vice-chairman of the Indiana Republican Party, while her husband was a member of the Indiana GOP who served as state banking commissioner. As Dwight W. Hoover, writes, 'Barr did not follow her husband into the Klan but instead led him.'[24] They made a formidable commercial force,

> On July 17, 1923, [Barr] signed a contract with the Klan to organize Indiana, Kentucky, West Virginia, Pennsylvania, Ohio, Michigan, New Jersey, and Minnesota. By terms of the contract she would receive one dollar for each woman initiated as a member after July 9, 1923. The initiation fee was not her sole reward. Because she headed the Women of the Ku Klux Klan in Indiana she also received four dollars for every member recruited… In return, she was supposed to act as the conduit for requests for robes sent to national headquarters. The sale of robes was a Klan monopoly that provided a considerable portion of the organization's funds.[25]

Barr's fortunes within the Klan were finally scuppered by accusations of embezzlement after the selling of KKK robes. *Indianapolis Times* journalist, George Dale, satirised her story in 1924, referring to Barr as the 'Quakeress Fakeress'. The satire seems to revolve around a familiar sort of 'critical misogyny' where the wrongdoing of a 'high powered' woman is raised as an example of women being especially manipulative – a 'klukerass', he writes, 'too fast for the feeble minded he-kluckers.'[26] The commercial form of the second KKK and the cultural flak that effervesces around this fascist movement – scandal, fraud, racketeering and grift – is particularly striking. Cults of celebrity, affiliate marketing, commercial contracts and a drive for subscribers were used to modulate rapid movement growth based on a sales call sheet that targeted existing white male Protestant fraternal organisations and women's clubs. Tyler and Clarke, public relations consultants, and lovers, meanwhile provided the advertising savvy the second Klan needed to go national. Tyler and Clarke agreed to do PR for the Klan in exchange for 80% of the $10 dues. Linda Gordon defines the second Klan as 'a for profit corporation... [A] huge moneymaking operation... People bought mansions, people bought yachts... [F]or the Klan, the profit motive was the highest order premise of what American greatness was so profiteering at first did not seem so reprehensible.'[27]

The rise of the second KKK also registers the take-off of the US culture industry and the role of evangelical churches in that development. Barr spoke at Indiana's Cadle Tabernacle, a 'megachurch', which eventually became home to a radio ministry in the 30s, reaching an estimated 30 million people from 1931 to the 1950s.[28] 'On an April evening in 1923,' Theo Anderson writes,

> Eighteen Ku Klux Klan members dressed in full regalia marched down the Tabernacle's center aisle and presented visiting evangelist E. J. Bulgin with a letter of appreciation and a check for $600 to be split between him and the Cadle Tabernacle Evangelistic Association. As the Klansmen filed out, the audience stood and applauded. That night 200 people reportedly converted to Christianity.[29]

Protestant white supremacy was already highly organised within the fraternal organisations that the Klan moved to unite under one monopoly venture. This provided the organisation with a market of subscribers and brand consumers that generated capital for next stage ventures, including in-house garment factories for maximising profit in industrial robe production, realty companies for investment in real estate and KKK life-insurance.[30] The second KKK was a prototype of commercial fascism that speaks to the intertwining of the 21st century fascism of the GOP and the 'Hustler Universities', crypto pyramids and social media subscription models of gender critical feminists, manosphere fascists, evangelical photo frame preachers and cult influencers. Yet balancing market positivity with a white supremacist rhetoric of the moral and cultural degenerations of markets proved complicated, as the organisation became overwhelmed by opportunism and scandal.[31]

Critically, the natalist emphasis on mothers as the natural agents of moral conservation was carried through into the KKK organising model along with temperance-style condemnation of *male immorality*. As well as the moral contamination and sexual perversion the Klan saw as emerging from Black people and immigrants, they also sought to provide an interventionist cure to the degraded eugenic health of the white race. As such, they attempted to enforce certain community standards among 'fallen' whites. Intimidation and violence were used against white men, and occasionally white women, for 'crimes' like adultery or premarital sex. Men deemed not to be adequately fulfilling their proper roles as husbands or fathers – whether due to alcohol abuse or a lack of patriarchal discipline – were routinely warned, then violently encouraged, to mend their ways. Such attacks often resulted from the denouncements and tip-offs of white women, Klan members or not. Of course, sexual violence by Klansmen, and white men more generally, was rampant – towards their wives, other white women and against Black women. David A. Horowitz's study of the Oregon KKK notes an ideological stress on 'personal revitalisation', male 'character building' and routine assessments of the 'moral character' of male members.[32]

The second KKK were reacting also to the 'mongrelization' (democratisation) of whiteness itself. US labour movements, white suffragists and white temperance leaders had deployed economic, nativist and natalist forms of white ethno-nationalism. The Knights of Labor combined big tent labourism with anti-immigration and anti-Chinese campaigns that were vicious and persistent.[33] However, some religious and ethnic lines (between white Europeans at least) began to blur around liberal democratic ideas of nationhood. By the 1920s, this assimilationist model of white supremacy, extending white status to Eastern and Southern Europeans, was blamed as part of a conspiracy to usurp the 'pioneer stock.' Hiram Evans, who ousted William Simmons as the national Klan's Imperial Wizard in 1922, wrote in 1926: 'Americanism can only be achieved if the pioneer stock is kept pure.'[34] He continued,

> There is more than race pride in this. Mongrelization has been proven bad. It is only between closely related stocks of the same race that interbreeding has improved men; the kind of interbreeding that went on in the early days of America between English, Dutch, German, Huguenot, Irish, and Scotch.[35]

This sentiment also turns up in cases where organised labour and the KKK were fraternising. Thomas R. Pegram notes how Midwest socialist agitator Morrison I. Swift argued in 1923 that despite 'rotten methods' the KKK were right to confront the 'amazing mongrel immigration' that furthered 'the decay of American stock.'[36]

The KKK platform brought the conspiratorial tradition of American nativism to the febrile atmosphere of the 1920s and gave it organisational teeth. The WKKK synthesised an era of women's suffrage and seismic changes in the social and political roles of women to carve out some autonomy in the white supremacist community. In doing so they underlined a defence of white homes and family life, the future of 'the race,' as even more fundamental to the aims of the KKK and tethered it that much more to the image of the American Dream. This example of a WKKK advert shows the kind of angle they used to recruit new members:

> Are you interested in the welfare of our Nation? As an enfranchised woman are you interested in Better Government? Do you not wish for the protection of Pure Womanhood? Shall

we uphold the sanctity of the American Home? Should we
not interest ourselves in Better Education for our children?
Do we not want American teachers in our American schools?
IT IS POSSIBLE FOR ORGANIZED PATRIOTIC WOM-
EN TO AID IN STAMPING OUT THE CRIME AND VICE
THAT ARE UNDERMINING THE MORALS OF OUR
YOUTH. The duty of the American Mother is greater than
ever before.[37]

A growth in divorce rates and women's increasing independence
impacted ideologies of the family. Moral panics that juxtaposed
commodification and moral denigrations of the nation and traditional gender roles parallel those of today. There was rapid commercial development in the manufacture of metropolitan brand
fashions, Black music and a rise in transgressive consumer trends.
Bootleggers humiliated the Prohibition agenda and rough trades
in erotica incensed movements for censorship.[38] The cultural
phenomena of economic and social change became the interface
for a commercialised KKK and WKKK to offer explanations and
solutions. They seized on 'threats' to nation, home and white
supremacy, following on from the relative success of populist
politicians before them, notably Georgia's antisemitic Senator
Tom Watson. The Klan stood for 'pure Americanism' and began
to recruit whole church congregations, social clubs and masonic
fraternities, who were wooed with generous donations, picnics,
church fairs, sports events, fireworks and cookouts.[39] The Klan
was, for a few years, a national movement with 'perhaps as high
as five million'[40] dues-paying members.[41] These dues were used
as capital for investment that including many failed ventures.
Mandatory KKK life insurance for members was an early idea
that never quite took off. However, recent research has shown
that a privately owned insurance company of the KKK, which
was intended to compete within the industry at large, was set
up in 1924. Despite supposed moral opposition to 'profiteering',
the second Klan had quickly adjusted to the spirit of the age. As
Miguel Hernandez explains,

In early 1924, Zeke E. Marvin, a highranking Texas Klansman and associate of Hiram Wesley Evans, attempted to revive the Klan's insurance scheme... [A]fter reading The International Jew, Henry Ford's infamous anti-Semitic thesis, he felt the need to create a life insurance company that could compete with the 'Jewish controlled companies' that dominated the market. To this end, the Imperial leadership founded the Empire Mutual Life Insurance Company in Kansas City, Missouri, with a capital stock of $100,000 and a surplus of $25,000. The company began advertising insurance policies in Texas and Missouri and claimed that in four months had sold close to $3,000,000 worth of stock. The scheme struggled to maintain itself due to the eventual decline of the Invisible Empire after 1925.[42]

Unlike their predecessors, the organisation prospered in the North and the West. Midwestern states like Pennsylvania, Michigan and Ohio were all strongholds. As were parts of New York, where young property heir Fred Trump, father of Donald, was once arrested, fully robed, on a Klan march in 1927.[43] Klan success on either side of the old Mason-Dixon line was indicative of a more general national reunification of white Protestantism.

American fascism

In its most successful Northern citadel, Indiana, it is estimated that between one quarter and one third of white men born in the state had been members at its zenith.[44] The flexibility of fascism, even when homogenised around a narrow white Protestant identity, is instructive here. According to Hiram Evans, the Klan was a tool for 'the common people ... to resume control of their country.'[45] Klansmen and women were solid members of local churches and even occasionally drawn from the ruling elite. More often, the KKK garnered (or forced) political backing from the highest echelons.[46] Debates continue as to its ideal types, but it is the regional tonality of Klan politics, the interfacing of non-violence and extreme violence, and its cross-class

compositions that are definitive. In her work on Athens, Georgia, MacLean stresses the appeal of the Klan to an economically insecure, petit bourgeois class fraction, rather than larger
manufacturers, farmers and other capitalist elites.[47] In Bentonville, Arkansas, however, it was the largest capitalist farmers,
the owners of the local orchards, not the subsistence farmers,
who were organising alongside local political leaders and law-
makers.[48] Klaverns, that is, local Klan halls, could include company managers, as well as skilled, often unionised, tradesmen,
who joined teachers, ministers, shop owners, salesmen, farmers,
veterans and housewives. The national KKK line was stridently
anti-communist and anti-union, but recent research has shown
some Klaverns to have been ideologically flexible, prepared to
make inroads into worker organisations and even support strikes
by white Protestant workers. In Midwest Akron, Ohio and deep
south Birmingham, Alabama, the KKK recruited white Protestant workers while attacking any small outcrops of multiracial
unionism. Pegram writes: 'Klan-sponsored Labor Day parades
were commonplace in midwestern strongholds… In Lansing,
Michigan a huge crowd of fifty thousand people celebrated
workers and the Klan on Labor Day in 1924.'[49] At the same time,
such alliances with labour were highly contingent. In Harrison,
Arkansas, in 1923, a Klan-supporting community faced off with
largely Protestant striking rail workers, breaking them up, ter-
rorising their families and lynching a strike supporter who dared
to shoot back. It was only after *this* event that Samuel Gompers
of the American Federation of Labor finally publicly condemned
the KKK, having resisted Black members' requests that he do so
earlier.[50]

The reach of the Ku Klux Klan escaped the attention of its
early historians, who largely considered it a fringe movement
only popular in insular towns and backwaters. This stereotypical
view was maintained until researchers began opening up surviving membership lists and exploring the extent of its regional
influence in northern states, cities, the Midwest and the South.
A 'populist' revision of the historiography has since held that in

fact the Klan was a mainstream civic organisation, with significant reach into state politics.[51] The KKK were mainstream for
a large and 'native' Protestant section of some states, hence its
appearance as something resembling a middle class social club.
But in other contexts, they mobilised vigilante and mob violence
or deployed intimidation tactics. Their 'populism' was based on
a limited appropriation of the people, their people. 'Reactionary
populism,' the definition offered by MacLean, coins the distinction. Demographic cross-sections of the Klan that are common
in specialist literature can sometimes elide a view of the activist
and leadership contingents within them. Some Klaverns, especially in the South, took a more extreme actionist outlook than
in the Midwest, where civic power was most organised. Police
involvement in vigilante actions, including murders, guaranteed
immunity from formal investigation (and formal records). This
begs the question of fascist mobilisation. Signs of fascism are often looked for on the street, but fascist mobilisation isn't always
visible. Fascist mobilisation that happens in border forces, police
departments and local community groups today, for instance,
has no intention of becoming apparent. The KKK, MacLean
maintains, was a movement operating 'between capital and un-
skilled labor' and organised around an animosity towards and
moral approbation of *both* labour and 'big business.'[52] Klan literature subscribed to a foreshortened, antisemitic analysis of capital
that like their fascist contemporaries in Europe, sought to elim-
inate class strife and to bring about a flourishing of white unity
in a purified nation.[53] MacLean, for this reason, offers a more
definitive view of the second Klan as an American fascist phenomenon, 'not only in its world view, but also in its dynamics as
a social movement, the Klan had much in common with German
National Socialism and Italian Fascism.'

It is an intriguing comparison, which may be helpful to un-
pack. The Nazis and the Klan shared similar myths of Northern
European white supremacy.[54] Yet the KKK were organising under very different social dynamics. First, the religious question
had not been overcome for American white supremacists in the

1920s. The KKK attacked Catholics because they believed Irish, Southern and Eastern European Catholics sullied whiteness.[55] These religious divisions were transcended in Europe by fascist theories of the *'volk'* in Germany or *'stirpe'* in Italy. Franco in Spain had managed to make Catholic elites hegemonic. America remained deeply divided along religious lines, not only due to migration histories, but because of market segmentation. The commodification of religion and the commercial power that competing churches brokered produced internal divisions within the evangelical tradition and between religions.[56] Secondly, the democratic terrain of early 1920s America was saturated with competing political interests. Catholic Italian-American and Irish-American elites had established power in US political parties, African-Americans were in their millions and developing significant militancy and forms of political representation, labour organisations were also developing a foothold in political parties through the mass expansion of industrial capital. Germany, by comparison, was bankrupt and had only just fought off a communist revolution. Italian liberal democracy was so weak that by 1922 the fascists could simply ignore it.[57] Squadistri took over train stations, postal services and other elements of the administrative state directly.[58] Thirdly, European fascist regimes took state power, whereas the KKK sank like a stone by the late 1920s. Yet the taking of state power from the liberal state can also be a misleading indicator for fascism. Paxton used an example of 'failed fascism' in France to argue that 'fascist interlopers cannot easily break into a political system that is functioning tolerably well. Only when the state and existing institutions fail badly do they open opportunities for newcomers.'[59] The second KKK, by comparison, took root within a flourishing democratic system and launched the careers of many fascists within it. Indeed, it was arguably because the American democratic and legal state was highly developed and ideologically adapted to rallying fascist causes that the second KKK pursued their politics democratically. By comparison, the Italian liberal state was underdeveloped. Italian fascists had introduced emergency legislation to close down elections by 1925. However, they struggled to implement fascist economic reforms because financial crisis forced them to conform to liberal economic orthodoxies.[60] There was also a rise in fraternal organisations but, unlike those in America, they grew sporadically to serve the needs of the Italian provinces. They were also ideologically ambiguous and deemed a possible threat to the fascist corporate state.[61] Far from being absolute, then, there was a civic society developing under Italian fascism that had relative autonomy from the power of the state.[62] Italian fascist elites were having to review their ideological hold over society, with new education programs, racial laws and imperial expansions.[63]

The KKK had a more organic relationship to American cultural life. Indeed, a race-based myth of anti-imperialism, first against the Crown, second against the Union, provided a fertile narrative of intergenerational 'Scotch-Irish' victimisation, which persists through the symbolism of the confederate flag.[64] The KKK had members in the police and local politics, as well as highly developed mass movement strategies and popular moral traditions to build upon. The expanded role of women in the KKK was also significant in this regard. While in Italy there were militant fascist women, some of whom joined the 'March on Rome' and participated in attacks on antifascists, they were small in number.[65] The second KKK meanwhile relied on politically active women throughout the organisation. Structured by strict hierarchies and chains of command similar to the male Klan's 'army,' the WKKK played a crucial role in reproducing the movement. There was an emphasis on Klanswomen as recruiters and on-the-ground strategists who gave 'the brand' legitimacy. A gendered focus on 'moral hygiene' was key as morality campaigns and front organisations were the KKK's best means of recruitment, alliance-building and burnishing its respectability.[66] As Blee writes, 'In some sense, the women's Klan posed few if any new political ideas. Rather, the WKKK consolidated and made exciting a political philosophy that had long penetrated movements for women's suffrage, temperance, and civic improvement.'[67] Whether their legitimacy was more down to a family-friendly image or the wider reactionary context is contestable, but unlike earlier and later Klan iterations, members in many parts of the country were less inclined to hide their membership or mask their faces.

Women of America, wake up!

Different motivations and political trajectories drew women to the KKK. Some were married or related to Klansmen but any assumption of straightforward male control over women's involvement would be wide of the mark. WKKK propaganda sought to enlist white American women to take action, to defend an American home and family life that was under siege. One poster read:

> Foreigners can live and make money where a white man would starve because they treat their women like cattle and their swarms of children like vermin, living without fear of God or regard for man... You should by voice and vote encourage for your husband's sake the restriction of immigration. Let us have fewer citizens and better ones. Women of America, wake up.[68]

Many Klanswomen had already been politically active, including in the two main parties, while 'some high-ranking WKKK leaders had also chaired local campaigns for suffrage.'[69] Many others joined through involvement in Protestant churches, especially the Baptist church. Numerous Klanswomen cut their political teeth in the WCTU or Anti-Saloon League (for whom Mary Elizabeth Tyler had previously worked, along with the Red Cross and Salvation Army). Across the country, Klanswomen, like MAGA women opposing 'CRT' or 'gender ideology' today, sat on school boards, helping to ensure continued racial segregation and attempting to get Catholic teachers banned from public schools. They led local boycotts against businesses owned by Black, Jewish or Catholic people. These campaigns were effective, especially in smaller towns, forcing isolated targets into bankruptcy and driving them out. Boycotts were aimed at larger targets: Hollywood movies, racialised as Jewish, and popular Black music and dancing, were singled out as alien poisons corrupting white youth. The Klan joined in a wider moral panic about sexually 'loose' youth culture and dance halls. Klansmen burned down buildings that hosted dances and conducted night patrols to intimidate young couples in parked cars.

The Klan's sheer combination of enemies made them vulnerable. Their racial vision was stricter and their membership more exclusive than other white supremacist formations. It was also stricter than the existing operations of structural racism. The KKK claimed to seek change through existing institutions while also being driven by extra-legal violence. Like much of today's US far right, they claimed to be the rightful inheritors of the traditions of the Founding Fathers and the Constitution. 'The Klan,' writes Blee, 'did more than simply mirror the bigotry of the majority population. It provided an organizational means to transform fears and resentments into political action.'[70] Walter White of the NAACP, a contemporary of the second Klan, wrote: 'The significance of such a movement is that the Klan was … the direct-action expression of a most dangerous doctrine of superiority which many Americans hold who are too respectable or too timid to translate it into violent action'.[71] State by state, Klan members built vote-winning strategies by sleuthing for immoral transgressions and wells of prejudice. Klan publications and speeches were infused with conspiracy; tales of Catholic plots, Jewish control and the need for 'pure Americans' to prepare for the coming 'race war.' Strongholds were often places where minority groups were particularly small in number and white Protestants were many, but this never fettered the imagination of what those minorities were up to. The Klan threatened labour organisers of French-speaking lumbermen in Lewiston, Maine, declared an end to 'machine politics' in Oakland, California, and bid to protect children from 'papal conspiracy' in Tillamook, Oregon.[72]

The second KKK developed a form of commercial fascism peculiar to the American racial regime, with the fraternal organisation functioning as a flexible organising unit. As Blee puts it, '[t]he Klan infused the culture of daily life with political content... Klannish political culture offered a way of life, a sense of purpose, and a worldview that drew on the ordinary racism and intolerance of white Protestant society.'[73] There was a cradle-to-grave, world-building breadth to the 1920s Klan unlike most far right movements have achieved in US history. This extended to creating its own time-world – it periodised a history with the US and the Klan at the centre of the universe. There were different names for the days of the week and months of the year, and an endless vocabulary of words beginning with the letter K. Klanswomen took the lead in organising gatherings – acting as the providers of care, friendship and white solidarity that knitted the movement together. Free nurseries and neighbourhood child care exchanges were developed, as was a caring infrastructure for members who fell ill. A Junior KKK was founded for teenage boys, a 'Tri-K-Klub' for teenage girls, while younger children had the 'Ku Klux Kiddies.'[74] The Klan leadership even tried and failed to establish a university. There were Klan christenings, funerals and weddings where brides kissed grooms before burning crosses with guests all decked out in Klan regalia. Social functions saw members strengthen ties with sports, singalongs and minstrel shows. The organisation of Klan social and sporting events operated not only at the local level but at state and national levels. Parades and marches demonstrated white pride, and white power, to the wider community. Camping trips were opportunities to showcase the militarism, masculinity and gender division the organisation prized. This tight-knit world could sometimes lead to a sense of alienation from aspects of wider society. Blee remarks that 'As a consequence of the absorption of the Klan into daily life, Klan members often found it difficult to comprehend negative reactions to the organization.'[75] The Klan at times referred to the outside world as the 'alien' world. Like gender criticals today, a highly cultivated sense of victimhood, of being misunderstood, can be perceived, with the sense of being brave truth-tellers in a world not yet ready to hear it. QAnon also offers a striking parallel to the second KKK, not only for its esoteric style, but a similar sense of coexisting missions: political campaigning, apocalyptic revivalism, religious crusades and money-making schemes. Gender critical and QAnon social media campaigns pestering politicians, celebrities and businesses, and harassing individuals, are not unlike the whispering and boycotting tactics of the Klan, whereby fearsome, infamous slander campaigns were used to destroy rival candidates. WKKK members used blackmail, character assassination and intimidation as well as an effective get-out-the-vote operation. These were the 'poison squads of whispering women', as Vivian Wheatcraft proudly termed them.[76] Wheatcraft was a leading Indiana Klanswoman who had long been an influential operator in that state's Republican party. Rival candidates were frequently denounced as being secret Jews or Catholics or as having shadowy connections. The influence of the Klan on politicians[77] was such that they 'managed to prevent either major party and all the nation's presidents in the decade from condemning it publicly.'[78]

Ideologies of gender and sex have always been central to the Klan's racial violence. Violence against racialised men (especially Black men) was justified on the basis of accused 'miscegenation.' Interracial marriage was anathema to all the Klan held dear. Jewish men were accused of plotting to abduct and pimp out white women *en masse*. Vigilante 'night-riding,' often condoned by local authorities, was deployed against racial targets, to enforce gender norms and protect the white nuclear family.[79] Still, the racism of the WKKK, the violence they embraced and perpetrated, doesn't lead us to simple conclusions about a clear-cut regression in their gender politics from the wider white women's movement. Most Klanswomen sought to assert *their rights* rather than their equality with white men. And in doing so they transgressed many gendered, middle class expectations just by being as politically active as they were. Klanswomen took up different positions on the role of women in society and in the Klan but fought an uphill struggle in a male-dominated organisation. There were ever-present tensions between KKK and

WKKK leaders and members over how much power Klanswom-
en should have. Similarly, today, far right women have spoken
out about the misogyny they face from their male comrades.[80]
Fascist online personality Tara McCarthy, for instance, tried to
call out alt-right men on Twitter in 2017: 'Men in the Alt Right
are going to have to decide whether they will continue to passive-
ly / actively endorse this behaviour, or speak out against it. If you
want more women speaking publicly about ethnonationalism, I
suggest you choose the latter.'[81] She later deleted the tweets and
locked her account.[82]

Resistance to the Klan and its afterlife

The KKK was pluralistic and 'populist' on one level as it was able
to bridge North / South and Democratic / Republican divides,
while enrolling suffragists and women organisers. But it was also
not short of enemies. The largest anti-Klan resistance emerged
in the early-mid 1920s in the Midwest states and New England.[83]
As Pegram writes, 'Anti-Klan violence brutally confirmed the reality of the ethnic and religious pluralism of the New Era, making the Klan's demand for a restricted American identity appear
as impossible as it was inflammatory.'[84] One Klan strategy, still a
staple of the far right today, was to march through immigrant
communities in order to provoke attacks. They hoped to paint
themselves as victims, and to focus attention on the violence
of their enemies and the attacks on their free speech, to garner
press sympathy and gain new members. At times this worked, at
other times it backfired. Depending on regional and local speci-
ficities, anti-Klan coalitions formed to organise counter-boycotts
of Klan-owned stores (or businesses that advertised in Klan publications) and mobilised forceful counter-demonstrations against
Klan parades.[85] Direct action attacks (with both sides armed)
ramped up in 1923 and 1924 to run the Klan out of town.[86] Violent anti-Klan mobilisations in those years in Ohio, Pennsylvania,
West Virginia, Delaware, New Jersey and Wisconsin invariably
emerged victorious, dealing a blow to Klan forces in those areas.
These were often led by first or second generation Irish, Italian,

Polish and Jewish immigrants, sometimes forming clandestine anti-Klan organisations of their own, such as the Knights of the Flaming Circle and the Knights of the Blazing Ring, who enjoyed lampooning the Klan and its rituals and costumes.[87]

A predominantly Catholic organisation that also had Black and Jewish leaders, the American Unity League (AUL), formed in Chicago in 1922. Inversely to the Klan, its membership was open to all *except* white Protestants. The AUL infiltrated local Klaverns or broke into Klan buildings to gain access to its membership rolls and revealed the names, addresses and professions of local Klan members in its newspaper, *Tolerance*. The slogan on the front of the paper's every weekly issue was 'Voicing a Protest Against Racial and Religious Discrimination.' These revelations had a big impact in Northern states, especially when prominent politicians, bankers and industrialists were revealed to be members. The AUL was thought to have been connected to a bomb in April 1923 that destroyed the Chicago office of the KKK journal *Dawn*.[88] The Klan were also attacked by gangsters and bootleggers for their prohibitionist stance.

The Black press and Black national organisations were very active against the Klan as its threat grew. Some focused on lobbying the authorities and arguing that the Klan was 'anti-American', while others emphasised the need for, and pointed to the already existing widespread practice of, Black self-defence. Many Black newspapers and journals expressed a certain cynicism or exasperation that other groups targeted by the Klan only became worried about racial or vigilante violence when it had begun to affect them.[89] The New York-based Black socialist monthly, *The Messenger,* kept a close eye on the Klan, covering it in nearly every issue throughout the early 1920s. In its 'Open Letter to America' about the KKK in its December 1920 edition, *The Messenger* lists the multiple targets of Klan violence – Black people, workers, Catholics, Jews, immigrants. Editors Chandler Owen and A. Philip Randolph compare the Klan to other reactionary forces around the world at that moment: the 'Black and Tans', the 'Fascisti of Italy', the 'Turk's massacres in Armenia', 'Leopold's atrocities in the Congo,' 'pogroms' against Jews in Eastern Europe. They call on unions and the Socialist Party, cultural organisations, radical and liberal publications, who they list by name, to condemn the Klan. They repeatedly refer to the Klan's strike-breaking function:

> We claim this is its objective and purpose. That is why it is financed by northern and southern capital jointly. That is why the government winks at it, colludes and connives at it ... and why the *New York Tribune* and the northern press ... is coddling and white-washing the Knights of the Ku Klux Klan.

Owen and Randolph call out Black politicians who kept silent on Klan terror, and skewered Black preachers and Marcus Garvey who inexplicably met with Klan leaders.[90]

The Messenger helped to organise large meetings and demonstrations with 'Irish, Jewish, German, Italian and Negro labor leaders and scholars.' In the September 1921 issue, they advocate the same kind of armed self-defence that they had previously called for in 1919, during the nationwide anti-Black riots of the 'Red Summer.'[91] They did so in the language of the 'New Negro', the masculine figure of the new Black generation, led by the African American men returning from war in Europe who refused to stand for being second class citizens. They wrote:

> Nor are the people wholly defenseless before these vandals and vile vultures. The law is that a man's house is his castle, that he may use sufficient force to repel an attack, and if he has reason to believe his life is endangered, he may kill! Now those white masks are not invulnerable. We haven't tried it, but we honestly believe a bullet will go through them.[92]

In November 1921, they outline a sort of antifascist vision for how to fight the Klan:

> As we very early insisted ... the Ku Klux Klan thieves and bootleggers must be fought by all against whom their darts are directed, plus all public spirited and far visioned persons.

The Klan announces that it is opposed to Negroes, Jews, Catholics, organized labor and foreigners. Then Negroes, Jews, Catholics, organized labor and foreigners should combine to annihilate the Klan. The Ku Klux Klan uses physical force. The Negroes, Jews, Catholics, labor and foreigners should use all the force necessary to suppress the Ku Kluxers.

'Negroes, Jews, Catholics, labor and foreigners,' they add,

Must not try to carry on any debating society. They must be prepared to protect themselves, must be well armed, must shoot to kill anyone who encroaches upon their lives. No tarring and feathering fraternity should be respected except by bullet, brick, bottle, club or some deadly and maiming weapon. A good cold steel lesson is what is needed.[93]

Significantly, in June 1922, *The Messenger* warned its readers that 'no sane, courageous thinker would contend that Negroes can afford to rely upon the police and authorities when the evidence reveals the police and authorities are largely members of the Klan.'[94]

The commercialisation of the Klan also left it vulnerable to disillusionment and splits. Their moral vigilantism, which aimed at keeping white Protestant patriarchal order in check, began to lose consensus support in some places. An inkling grew that it was more geared towards settling local scores than godly rectitude. Slowly, scattered state actors summoned the gumption to enforce some laws against Klan violence, aided by growing numbers of ex-Klan members willing to testify against their former comrades. Major public scandals multiplied and fatally weakened the organisation nationally. The WKKK and KKK were characterised throughout their high period (1921-24) by constant infighting, power struggles, legal wrangles and money-grabbing. This resulted in a haemorrhaging of members in the second half of the decade. It was a commercial operation that many KKK purists became disillusioned with.[95] And this demise was punctuated by the horrific 1925 rape and murder of Madge Oberholtzer by Indiana grand dragon, D.C. Stephenson. Stephenson bit Oberholtzer countless times on the back (wounds that contributed to her death by bacterial infection); an outrage that starkly contradicted the Klan's propagated image of male chivalry and moral reform.[96] What is resoundingly clear, however, is that far right and fascist surges always have an afterlife. Some members thought the second Klan wasn't male or violent enough. They went and formed vigilantist groups in the mould of the first.[97] Many Klanspeople and sympathisers went on to have successful careers and live respectable middle class lives.[98] Many Klanswomen remained politically active long after the Klan folded, including in the two main parties, living long, normal, white lives, remembering with pride and nostalgia the friends they had made in the Klan.[99]

The violence of the Klan had significant and lasting impacts on racial segregation and urban demography that for some families spanned the generations. In a remarkable series of oral history interviews (from the 1970s to the 2000s) with elderly Jewish, Catholic and Black citizens of Muncie, Indiana, interviewees born around 1900-1930 recall their experience of the Klan. One woman, born in 1902, who remains anonymous, recalls the reason their family of three generations came to Indiana from Kentucky,

> My grandmother used to sit down on the floor and tell me about it… [S]he says that they'd ride up on horses, go in colored people's homes and shoot 'em down like dogs – ride out and leave 'em dead. So that's the reason why they moved from Kentucky, on that account, Ku Klux Klan.[100]

From the first KKK in 19th century Kentucky to the second KKK of early 20th century Muncie, Indiana,

> They had a skatin' rink out there… I had two sons. And I'd go out there and watch the kids dance and skate. So, Clarence Benadum, he used to be a lawyer here in Muncie … bringing them [Ku Klux Klan] to Muncie … they set the building on

fire and burned it down to the ground.[101]

A Jewish educator, Kenneth Davis, provides some insight into local attorney Benadum,

> He probably was the most archetypal anti-Semite kind of Klan, like anyone would possibly think of. But it's kind of ironic, in that presently I am now living in his house. When we first moved here and looked, you know, to the basement and some of the areas that don't always get full attention when someone moves out, we found some old copies of his broadsheet, *The X-ray*.[102]

Rachel Lipp, whose Jewish family left Germany in the 1850s, recalls that she was 'was too young to realize too much about the Klan, but I do know that that's why I was taken out of Muncie and put in school at St. Mary of the Woods.'[103] Sister Jean Perry, a Catholic, interviewed in 2006, recollects,

> The other thing that I always remember as a kid was the big 'KKK' imbedded in the cement outside our school, and why they never got rid of that. But it was like we knew the Ku Klux Klan had some hold in Muncie. I didn't know what it was at the time, but I knew that it was not good for Catholics and that somebody was making a statement to us.[104]

Lucille Williams, who is described by the interviewer as 'long active in Negro women organizations', describes the entrenchment of Jim Crow laws of segregation that were previously poorly enforced,

> Then you could, you could feel the change. Before that time you, you did not have a feeling of segregation... [W]hen the Ku Klux Klan came into Muncie and, well... [Y]ou could feel the difference in the community after the organization of the Ku Klux Klan.[105]

3. Moral Purity and the Suffragettes

Feminist revivals of sex essentialism in Britain have often initiated a return to the 19th century suffrage inheritance. Radical feminist Sheila Jeffreys was writing sympathetic histories of Victorian purity feminism in the 1990s and was criticised at the time by feminist historian and lesbian feminist Margaret Hunt for evading critical commentary of the 'moral repressiveness' of social purity. Hunt wrote, 'Jeffreys' way of doing history tells us a great deal about her feminism.'[1] This was before Jeffreys moved towards being more openly transphobic in the late 1990s and into the 2000s. The British gender critical movement continues to revise and innovate this identification with the 19th century women's cause. Indeed, gender critical campaigners repeat sex essentialist feminist maxims of the 19th century as if they are principles of an ancient and essential truth. As Sally Hines cautions: 'At the hub of this battle is the sex/gender binary wherein "sex" is reinstated as the primary source of women's oppression in order to agitate against trans rights. More so, reproductive function has gained primacy as the fundamental site of women's disadvantage.'[2] Hines argues that colonial sex essentialist contents are revitalised through the gender critical movement:

> A project of trans decolonisation thus starts with a critique of Western and white gender theory and seeks to explore the impact that colonialism, racism and whiteness have had on the gendered understandings and practices of indigenous peoples and people of colour.[3]

As we noted in the introduction to this book, many feminists have argued that gender critical ideology is not feminist at all and there are valid reasons to insist on this. Some gender critical influencers in Britain live in castles and many have experience and confidence manoeuvring within corridors of power. This means they are able to dominate discourse via a fawning media most of the time. They are not being imprisoned for their beliefs. Courts have at times upheld the right of transphobic individuals to discriminate because individuals within the media, legislature and political executive not only hold transphobic beliefs, but are concerned with policing and marshalling cisnormativity and re-productive rights. Unlike the British 19th century feminist move-ment, which we will look at now, much of the state, the news media and most of the church is already behind most gender critical stances and logic today – nobody needs winning over.[4] In this sense, Mallory Moore argues, 'holding an oppressive ideolo-gy is indistinguishable from just following and reproducing the existing disciplinary practices of wider society.'[5] While there are examples of personal and social consequences faced by the most rabid gender critical campaigners,[6] most leading gender critical feminists are 'cancelled' only to reappear on the front pages of tabloids and broadsheets. This is an ideology of elites. Yet re-fusing gender criticals the moniker of feminism because of the reactionary forces this movement assembles also risks ennobling historical feminism, which was formed through popular and elite networks with religious, as well as reactionary associations. We have explored links between the American constitutional struggles of the 19th century and fascism in the 1920s through the prevalent movement paradigms of the women's cause. We look now at the relationship between women's suffrage, social purity feminism, class struggle and Ireland in the British imperial setting.

We never get out of the hands of men

Just as US suffragists were in part mobilised by the codification of women's disenfranchisement by the Reconstruction Amend-ments, there is a similar story in Britain. Sylvia Pankhurst wrote, 'The [Reform] Act of 1832, by employing the term "male per-son", for the first time in English history, expressly debarred women from exercising the franchise it created.'[7] This exclusion was confirmed in the 1867 Act. Sylvia wrote of this early period: 'The women's movement ... passed from timidity to timidity.'[8] This begins with the participation of middle-class women in religious movements and institutions from the 1820s onwards. Middle class religious sisterhoods in the 1850s educated many women, with some becoming relatively self-determined community organisers and intellectuals, especially within the Anglican church. Anglican Church Congresses, instigated in 1861, then offered members a conference circuit where women began to organise into sections and give lectures. Small suffrage groups developed around these civic and religious networks.[9] They lobbied power-brokers, unsuccessfully trying to plot legal routes to enfranchisement. Nevertheless, women became more active in the religious missions and civic institutions of parish life. In the 1860s, missions such as the Salvation Army recruited thousands of working-class women into their ranks of ordained Army Clergy. By the 1880s, reforms saw women gain local franchise rights and be elected as Poor Law guardians, ie middle-class women were democratically empowered to administer the poverty of working-class women. The breakthrough was swift. According to Anne Digby, 'by 1900 there were over 1,000 female guardians, and twenty years later there were over 2,000 of them in the local state.'[10] Phillipa Levine argues that there was also some contingency regarding class. The cruel instrumentality of new poor law reforms could not always be enforced as statesmen envisioned. The regionalisation of the parish into poor unions still relied on personal motivation and ideological consensus within the middle class to exact punishments. There is evidence that some women were motivated to alleviate some of that cruelty. Levine shows that some of the middle class married women who took Poor Law Guardian roles also sought universal free school dinners for the poor or campaigned to ban the cane.[11]

British abolitionist cliques, suffrage movements and social purity movements were largely independent of one another but had overlapping themes and floating memberships. Not unlike US temperance movements, social purity movements in Britain began attracting churchwomen to the women's cause. The moral association of vice and alcohol consumption took on a similar complexion, but prohibition was a secondary issue in Britain. The driving issue for social purity reformers was the sexual basis of male power and issues of sexual morality. Inspiration was found in the successful repeal of the Contagious Diseases (CD) Acts, which 'legislated for compulsory, periodic sanitary examinations of women suspected of being prostitutes in garrison towns and ports throughout England.'[12] This series of invasive measures was introduced in the 1860s as an attempt by the state to confront the rise of venereal disease in the army. In a fascinating regional study of two English ports, Plymouth and Southampton, historians Judith R. Walkowitz and Daniel J. Walkowitz, show how repressive policing of sex workers subject to CD registration mandates, drew solidarity from the street, 'the C.D. Acts were very much a reality of street life. On Cross Street, on Central Street and on Granby Streets, crowds would gather to witness women being dragged off for examination and were known to intervene in [sic] their behalf.'[13] Many of these women were sex workers, some were not, or were sex workers between seasonal clothing trades to support the maritime and naval industry. Some women in Plymouth had migrated because of a collapse of trades in Cornwall and greater Devon and set up independently around the docks. Besides, as the Walkowitzs write, 'factors other than economic necessity may well have attracted young women to prostitution: independence from family control and a greater social and cultural freedom generally. The desire to break away from parental influence.' Sexual promiscuity within the working classes 'meant certain forms of prostitution may not have represented a striking departure from accepted mores.'[14] Unmarried women who were sex workers, also lived with male partners, and were sometimes dragged into 'lock' hospitals, with their partners left to visit them from behind guarded hospital walls. Resistance to the CD Acts often therefore manifested as an anti-detention struggle, as women taken by the police fought to escape wards. Riots broke out in courtrooms as a more general anti-police sentiment emerged in reaction to the increase in monitoring and sexual surveillance the CD acts brought to working class communities around the ports and docklands. A woman, testifying to Josephine Butler, one of the more radical reformers and a slavery abolitionist, described the misogynistic enterprise:

> It is men, men only men, from the first to the last, that we have to do with! To please a man I did wrong at first, then I was flung about from man to man. Men police lay hands on us. By men we are examined, handled, doctored and messed on with. In the hospital it is a man again who makes prayers and reads the Bible for us. We are had up before magistrates who are men, and we never get out of the hands of men.[15]

The CD acts were repealed by 1883 due to the combined resistance of the women themselves, progressive lawyers, women abolitionists and a mix of campaigners. The suffrage movement had kept some distance from the CD Acts for fear they would stigmatise women. However, it soon became clear that questions of individual liberty and the individual rights of women as equal to men were inseparable from the issues contained within it. Key campaigners for repeal had gained the support of John Stuart Mill, whose *Subjection of Women* remains a major index of arguments for women's rights. Mill's intervention into the CD Acts provides us with fascinating clarity about how far the universal principles of liberty could stretch. Mill opposed the laws, as they took away 'the security of personal liberty ... almost entirely from a particular class of women intentionally, but incidentally and unintentionally, one may say, from all women whatever.'[16] However, women subject to similar measures across the Empire had not previously roused the philosophical interest of Mill, who worked for 35 years for the East India Company (EIC) before publishing his major works.[17] As Eileen Hunt Botting and Sean Kronewitter argue, the CD Acts formalised regulations of sexuality that had already been enforced in the colonies:

Even within the empire, official regimes of regulation already existed, such as in Malta … and in Hong Kong from 1857, and from the early eighteenth century, various sanitary measures (including the establishment of Lock Hospitals) to combat venereal and other sexual diseases had been implemented in Penang, and then later in other parts of the Straits Settlements, and in Yogyakarta.[18]

In *On Liberty*, Mill wrote, 'we may leave out of consideration those backward states of society in which the race itself may be considered as in its nonage.'[19]

Women from 'barbarian' societies remained in a primitive state and had not yet developed the 'maturity of their faculties,' as Mill put it.[20] However, for the civilised, 'legal subordination of one sex to another … is wrong in itself.'[21] Middle class reformers saw that if sex workers could have their right to liberty defended by Mill and British soldiers blamed for 'communication' between them (Mill even argued that the men, not the women, should be inspected) then all women nationally were set to benefit. Inspired by the repeal of the CD acts, campaigners in the 1880s would therefore broaden the issue of sexual morality to target men who were sexually immoral. What came to be known as the 'double standard' helped reformers to turn public candour on victims of male promiscuity, child abuse and prostitution. Brothels were publicly and spectacularly targeted to save women, who were simply cleared off the street. As Judith Walkowitz documents,

> London police found themselves increasingly under pressure from social purity and antivice groups to suppress the indoor resorts of West End prostitutes – Cremorne Gardens, the Argyll Rooms, the Holborn dancing casino, the infamous nighthouses at Haymarket – as well as to clear public thoroughfares and theaters of streetwalkers to make room for respectable women.[22]

These campaigns were abstracted from the radical working class and cross-class pluralities that characterised resistance to the police, courts, hospitals and volunteer associations that formed a repressive network through the CD acts. Interestingly, however, much like 'groomer' conspiracism and anti-sex work feminism today, the purity reformers generated florid and voyeuristic anti-elites content to promote their cause. After the repeal of the CD acts, Butler and Catherine Booth of the Salvation Army approached the journalist W.T. Stead to assist their campaign to raise the age of consent from 13 to 16 and to 'punish traffickers in vice.' Judith R. Walkowitz calls Stead's 'Maiden Tribute of Modern Babylon' 'one of the most successful pieces of scandal journalism published in Britain during the 19th century.'[23] The 'Maiden Tribute,' Walkowitz writes, 'documented the sale of "five pound" virgins to aristocratic old rakes, graphically describing the way … "daughters of the people" had been "snared, trapped and outraged either when under the influence of drugs or after a prolonged struggle in a locked room."'[24] This lurid style juxtaposed perfectly with bumbling speeches in Parliament that revealed a lack of urgency around the issue, and often some personal ease with prostitution as a rite of passage for young ruling class men. The scandal built to a crescendo as Hyde Park saw 250,000 out in protest to demand passage of the legislation that Butler, Booth and others were lobbying for. Walkowitz describes some of the attendees:

> Members of the Ladies National Association for the Repeal of the Contagious Diseases Acts, dressed in black, arrived in carriages, while 'from another part of town' came the members of the Women Trade Unions and employees of the Army Clothing Establishments, led by Henrietta Muller, followed along by wagonloads of young virgins dressed in white, flying the banner 'Innocents will they be slaughtered.'[25]

On trade union and socialist protest banners 'appeared skilled workingmen with the tools of their craft, or as Herculean figures, endowed with classical bodies; while women only materialized either as bereft widows, deserving of fraternal protection, or as inspiring angels of justice and socialism.'[26]

Purity feminism

This protest pushed the legislation over the line and proved the expediency of a popular style of 'government by journalism' that Stead saw as an answer to the detachment of parliament from the voice of the people.[27] Stead innovated a 'new journalism' in the 1880s that had an unparalleled impact on the Victorian politics of sexual morality.[28] Indeed, the Hyde Park protest was a popular movement event that was attended by the working classes as well as reformer institutions. Yet as with carceral anti-sex work feminism today, the politics of such legislation locked victims into their conditions and separated them from the cultures of solidarity that sex workers and the working class had developed over time. Walkowitz writes,

> The 'Maiden Tribute' not only mapped out the same social geography as late-Victorian pornography; it also replicated, in a moralizing frame, many of the sadistic scenarios that filled pornography's pages. Simultaneously, it established a continuity with some of the themes of sadistic hunting and instrumental rape raised in women's fiction and Butler's feminist propaganda.[29]

The implications were wide ranging and significantly repressive. Legislation designed to protect women from 'white slavery' and bring elite gentlemen to justice manifested in the policing of sex workers, children, the working class and gay men. Walkowitz:

> The public furore over the 'Maiden Tribute' forced the passage of the Criminal Law Amendment Act of 1885, a particularly nasty and pernicious piece of omnibus legislation. The 1885 Act raised the age of consent for girls from 13 to 16, but it also gave police far greater summary jurisdiction over poor working-class women and children – a trend that Butler and her circle had always opposed. Finally, it contained a clause making indecent acts between consenting male adults

a crime, thus forming the basis of legal prosecution of male homosexuals in Britain until 1967. An anti-aristocratic bias may have prompted the inclusion of this clause (reformers accepted its inclusion but did not themselves propose it), as homosexuality was associated with the corruption of working-class youth by the same upper-class profligates, who, on other occasions, were thought to buy the services of young girls. Despite the public outcry against corrupt aristocrats and international traffickers, the clauses of the new bill were mainly enforced against working-class women, and regulated adult rather than youthful sexual behaviour. Between 1890 and 1914, the systematic repression of lodging house brothels was carried out in almost every major city in Great Britain. In many locales, legal repression dramatically affected the structure and organisation of prostitution. Prostitutes were uprooted from their neighbourhoods and had to find lodgings in other areas of the city. Their activity became more covert and furtive. Cut off from any other sustaining relationship, they were forced to rely increasingly on pimps for emotional security as well as protection against legal authorities. Indeed, with the wide prevalence of pimps in the early 20th century, prostitution shifted from a female- to a male-dominated trade. Further, there now existed a greater number of third parties with a strong interest in prolonging women's stay on the streets. In these and other respects, the 1885 Act drove a wedge between prostitutes and the poor working-class community. It effectively destroyed the brothel as a family industry and centre of a specific female subculture; further undermined the social and economic autonomy of prostitutes; and increasingly rendered them social outcasts.[30]

Walkowitz shows how the working class were broken into respectable shapes and rough pieces by the social reformers. Butler didn't want overzealous police surveillance of working-class women and girls, but that was the result. Aristocrats may have been the target of lurid journalism but remained untouched by the legislation. The interest of the purity reformer was in scandalising men into action and chastity. Yet Stead wrote from the perspective of a male voyeur, who solicited sex, before pulling back at the final moment. Media historian Gretchen Soderland writes, 'while purity movements attempted to convince men to turn away from vice, Stead's report linked the seemingly contradictory affective states of lust and moral outrage. Rescue itself, it must be acknowledged, is also a powerful sexual fantasy.'[31] 'Maiden's Tribute' landed at the bourgeois man's breakfast table daily, with titles such as 'The Violation of Virgins' and 'Strapping Girls Down'. This initial enterprise of carceral feminism provided its textbook case. Walkowitz writes, 'although female victimisation was a sincere concern of feminists, it also served diverse political interests... [A]nti-feminists used the occasion to activate men into a new crusade to protect rather than emancipate women – a crusade that was, at times, overtly misogynist.'[32]

The Ladies Association for the Care of Friendless Girls was set up by social purity leader Ellice Hopkins in 1883 and was ready to intern and reform these women. Redolent of anti-porn and anti-sex worker feminism in our own time, Hopkins campaigned to rescue prostitutes from their sinful activities. She called for the policing of pornographic materials and pushed for the state to take away young girls, for their own protection, from poor or incompetent parents. Reports of rural promiscuity from upstanding Christian women were answered by Hopkins with leaflets and advice, including 'supervision of after-school leisure activities, Sunday School trips and choir excursions.'[33] She also played to the heartstrings of church elites. Testimonies from those who met Hopkins claim she once moved two Anglican Bishops to tears after skilfully relaying stories of 'fallen' women.[34]

Hopkins contributed to male purity sessions for miners, as well as students in elite universities.[35] She set up the White Cross Army, also in 1883, with the help of the Bishop of Durham to fulfil this intention. Unlike public school statesmen, Hopkins was prepared to fraternise with working class men, visiting and lecturing in pubs. 'Whilst her husband goes to the public-house and gets drunk,' she wrote, 'it is very hard for her to go to church and get pious.' If the men should have to go to the pub, Hopkins insisted,

> Some local doctor should display gorgeously-coloured dia-grams of the results of drinking to the internal organs, the inflammation being emphasized by much expenditure of vermillion; statistical statements should be made, both gen-eral and local, of the amount of money spent in drink, and what the money might effect if spent on their own homes.[36]

Her aperture for social purity was empire wide. In her 1899 book, *The Power of Womanhood; or Mothers and Sons*, Hopkins expanded her vision of morality, empire and the transatlantic movements of purity:

> The British Empire, the great American Republic, the two greatest civilizing, order-spreading, Christianizing world power ever known, can only be saved by a solemn league and covenant of her women to bring back simplicity of life, plain living, high thinking, reverence for marriage, chivalrous re-spect for all womanhood, and a high standard of purity for men and women alike.[37]

In *Beyond The Pale: White Women, Racism and History*, Vron Ware shows the importance of just such family and race discourses in the ideology of British imperialism and the role of early British feminism within it:

> It was not just as mothers that British women performed a central role in maintaining the Empire: the ideology of white womanhood, structured by class and race, embraced women in all their familial roles. Whether as Mothers of the Empire or Britannia's Daughters, women were able to symbolize the idea of moral strength that bound the great imperial family together. In their name, men could defend that family in the same spirit as they would defend their own wives, daughters or sisters if they were under attack.[38]

Many purity reformers thought penal reform for sinful women was the means to realise this civilising mission. Hopkins was a cross-class fraterniser and firmly rejected this notion, as she wrote:

> As things are now men divide us women into two classes; us pure women for whom nothing is too good, and those others for whom nothing is too bad... [L]et us prove by our actions that our womanhood is ONE; that a sin against our lost sisters is a sin against us.[39]

Suzanne Elisabeth Morgan offers a sympathetic account of Hopkins' religious and moral intentions based on the universality she was able to devise through sex essentialist notions of womanhood. Indeed, it's important not to reduce Hopkins to a caricature of the pious reformer whose actions were purely intended to discipline working class women (even if this was the effect of social purity). What really differentiated Hopkins from other social reformers was her ability to select and use victims for reform purposes rather than simply exact punishment. If men persisted in using working-class women as instruments for sex, Hopkins would show purity and suffrage campaigners how they could instrumentalise them as victims. This has since become a representational motif of the secular public sphere. It is an element of the campaign footings of liberal feminism and anti-sex work campaigns, with regressive and violent consequences for working class women, especially sex workers.

An imperial split

Tracing the divergent paths taken by members of Britain's leading suffragist family, the Pankhursts, gives us a useful perspective on womanhood as an identity formed by colonialism and imperialism. It also underlines that the demand for suffrage alone was no clear indicator of political content. Indeed, we cannot stress enough how contingent the content was. The horizon of Emmeline and Christabel Pankhurst's ambitions became the enfranchisement of women like them. They envisioned little change to women's roles in society, not to mention the lives of women colonised and exploited across the Empire. Nonetheless, within a few years of its founding in 1903, the Pankhursts' Women's Social and Political Union (WSPU) grew to be an impressive, highly centralised organisation. It was elitist, hierarchical and dominated by Christabel and Emmeline. It raised huge sums through donations and its newspaper had a circulation of 40,000, and it could mobilise huge numbers for demonstrations. By 1910, it had 110 salaried staff and 'an income and central offices far exceeding those at the disposal of the Labour Party.'[40] Christabel wrote: 'There can be no mating between the spiritually developed women of this new day and men who in thought and conduct with regard to sex matters are their inferiors.' The feminist paper, *The Woman's Signal*, declared in 1894 that this was a rebellion 'that is Puritan and not Bohemian … an uprising against the tyranny of organized intemperance, impurity, mammonism, and selfish motives.' The imperialist centering of women as moral bearers of the nation was developed as a site of tactical interest for Suffragettes who were interested in 'deeds, not words.'

The direct action the Suffragettes are known for began in 1909 with campaigns of window-breaking and other criminal damage (including large scale attacks on property and the targeting of high-ranking politicians). This garnered mass publicity and condemnation (including from other suffragist groups and labour movement organisations), not to mention ferocious police violence. Titillating press coverage was captivated and horrified by Suffragette violence, as it subverted expectations of how middle-class Edwardian women were supposed to behave. The tactics led to many stints in prison for the Pankhursts and dozens of other women who conducted sleep, thirst and hunger strikes, often being force-fed by the state. Sylvia later critiqued this strategy: 'the movement required not more serious militancy by the few, but a stronger appeal to the masses to join the struggle.'[41] She rejected vanguardism at the expense of coalition-building and deeper organising: 'Secretly planned militancy was a method of desperation adopted in the hope of shortening the longer struggle.'[42] The strategic shift from lobbying to what would now be called terrorism complicates the Suffragette image. Respectable, nationalist memorials today cynically emphasise the *legalistic* results of their campaigns. As with much memorialisation, historical figures and movements are open to wide ranging identifications in the present. The Suffragettes' actual confrontations with state and property, however, were also not incommensurable with their allegiances to the nation. Indeed, splits formed within the WSPU over national questions. The imperialist loyalties of the WSPU took on a more defined character from 1912-1917 when the Home Rule crisis, war with Germany and the Easter Rising split a suffrage movement that had been able to forge fragile alliances across British and Irish organisations. This period of division offers interesting parallels with gender critical modes of political expediency. Especially their adoption of a strategic footing that is notionally indifferent to colonial and national realities but ultimately rests on the backing of an imperialist state.

The troubled alliance between the WSPU and the Irish Women's Franchise League (IWFL), set up in Dublin in 1908, encapsulates the colonial stresses of the prewar conjuncture. The IWFL was founded with the aim of establishing women's suffrage within any Home Rule legislation. It had always collaborated with the WSPU but, as Margaret Ward explains, 'harmonious relations between British and Irish feminists began to falter once the Home Rule issue began to dominate political life.'[43] Parliamentary deal-making, not unlike the US Republican manoeuvrings during the politics of Reconstruction, was a catalyst. The Liberal Party had won the 1910 general election with support from the Irish Party. Prime Minister H. H. Asquith was sympathetic to Home Rule, but a determined opponent of women's suffrage. John Redmond, Irish Party leader, pledged support to Asquith by opposing suffrage and hoped this would help Ireland with the Home Rule Bill. Christabel reacted with fury, declaring war on the Irish Party and dedicating organisational activities to opposing Home Rule. As a result, Irish women suffragists were pulled into a matrix of hostilities not unlike the position of African American women during the explosive AERA conferences in the first chapter. The resulting WSPU slogan, 'No Votes For Women, No Home Rule,' Ward explains, 'was a tactic which had unfortunate repercussions within Ireland because it could be readily adopted by women who believed in the Unionist cause, using feminist-inspired arguments as a further tactic to stall Home Rule.'[44] A bad situation was made worse when the WSPU decided to disrupt Home Rule negotiations in Ireland. Ward writes,

> In July 1912, three members of the WSPU arrived in Dublin in pursuit of Prime Minister Asquith, who was visiting Ireland in order to reassure the people of his determination to push through the Home Rule Bill… After a small hatchet was thrown and an attempt made to burn down the Theatre Royal, venue for the Asquith meeting, the women were arrested. Their actions were received with great hostility in Ireland and reactionary organizations like the Ancient Order of Hibernians made this the pretext for verbal and physical assaults on suffragists each time they organized public meetings that summer.[45]

Before the outbreak of war in 1914, the WSPU were prepared to play fast and loose with Ireland based on parliamentary arithmetic. They were indifferent as to the impact this had on their Irish comrades. Katelyn Burns reported on an interface between British gender critical feminists and trans-inclusive Irish organisers a century later:

> During the Irish referendum on abortion rights in 2018, some British gender-critical feminists withheld support for campaigners who supported abortion rights, citing the trans supportive attitudes of Irish feminism, going so far as to schedule an anti-trans meeting in Dublin at the height of the campaign season. Irish feminists responded with a scathing open letter

denouncing the event and reaffirming their support for the womanhood of trans women.[46]

Irish Party opposition to suffrage had shown Christabel that '[Irish] nationalist Members hold the fate of the Suffrage cause for the whole kingdom in their hands.' This was reason enough for Christabel to expand into Ireland and set up WSPU branches under her direct command. The prospect of British women taking over the Irish women's cause produced considerable consternation for native feminists. Christabel wrote to the IWFL to reassure them that good relations would be maintained: 'it is not nationality but personality that counts.' Ward comments on the ironic reception of this letter from the IWFL, 'Hannah Sheehy-Skeffington's initial response was to write a huge exclamation mark in ink beside the final sentence: "We are all one in the women's suffrage faith."'[47]

Christabel's autocratic style led to internal splits within the British organisation and estrangement of Irish nationalist Suffragettes in particular. She had long dismissed the more revolutionary aspirations of working-class women. Her younger sister Sylvia was moving in the opposite direction. She founded the East London Federation of Suffragettes (ELFS) in 1912, a large working-class movement rooted in London's radical East End, which had, 'by 1917 ... 30 branches nationwide (the majority in the East End), capable of mobilising thousands of women.'[48] Sylvia was finally expelled from the WSPU in 1914 for aligning more and more with socialist causes. She was particularly censured by Christabel for publicly showing solidarity with Irish trade unionists in the famous Dublin lock-out. Her political differences with her sister and mother were profound and grew more so as they went their separate ways, remaining estranged for the rest of their lives.

Sylvia founded one of the great radical newspapers of the period which she edited for a decade. The changing name of the paper – from *Woman's Dreadnought* to *Workers' Dreadnought* – showed the changing ideological basis and political focus of Sylvia and her comrades. Unlike other newspapers in Britain, the *Dreadnought* defied censors to demand that soldiers refuse to fight in the war and published letters written by serving soldiers who intended to desert. The paper's offices were later raided for this act.[49] ELFS led anti-war campaigns, rent strikes, and practical organising to share the burdens of local women left without husbands, food or income. According to her son Richard: 'During the first years of the war [Sylvia] established the Mothers' Arms, a maternity clinic and Montessori school, and four other clinics, two cost-price restaurants, and a co-operative toy factory designed to provide work for persons unemployed on account of the conflict. She also founded the League of Rights for Soldiers' and Sailors' Wives and Relatives, to work for better pensions and allowances.'[50] The women of ELFS' feminist focus was undiminished by a turn towards revolutionary class struggle as the whole movement was impacted by the Russian Revolution. Women's rights campaigners took up positions for or against the Revolution as political trajectories diverged wildly through times of upheaval. ELFS organised demos demanding equal pay, prison reform and an end to 'sweating' labour, with trade union collaboration – especially East End dockers, many of whom were married to ELFS women.

To the race as well as the family

In 1914, when war broke out, the WSPU continued its march rightwards and its offices were disbanded in Ireland. Emmeline and Christabel rebranded as the 'Women's Party,' rechristening their *Suffragette* newspaper *Britannia*. The Pankhursts' setting up of a 'Women's Party' bought into a wider notion that there was such a thing as a 'women's vote,' that women as a section of society could be approached electorally as a homogenous interest group. It had all but folded by the end of 1919. Emmeline and Christabel suspended all suffrage activities, subordinating themselves to the war effort and advocating women's war work, believing that 'the eventual reward for such loyalty would be the parliamentary vote.'[51] Christabel demanded mass conscription from the earliest stage, and called for wholesale internment of male and female aliens of 'enemy blood', including those born in Britain to German parents,[52] as well as their exclusion from the civil service and a ratcheting of deportations. Her pro-war zealotry was McCarthyesque, with diatribes against 'weak' members of the Cabinet. In a language that shows continuity with earlier movements focused on moral purity and concerned with contagion, she wrote: 'I consider the Pacifists a disease … a very deadly disease,' excoriating anyone who so much as flinched at anything less than the total destruction of the German enemy.[53] *Britannia* was equally horrified by the Russian Revolution. Emmeline advocated armed intervention as a solution. After the war, low on funds and desperately needing them to raise the four baby girls she had adopted, Pankhurst, now in her 60s, embarked on a speaking tour of North America. Touring at a time when the second Klan was on the rise, Emmeline's speeches focused on topics that were equally important to the WKKK. She regaled crowds about how 'the great work confronting the women now is the suppression of Bolshevism.'[54] She spread awareness about the dangers to race, nation and Empire, of venereal disease and prostitution.

Once David Lloyd George's muscular government took power during World War One, it received the full backing of Emmeline and Christabel. This was quite the turnaround from four years earlier when Suffragettes had attempted to bomb his house. It is known that Lloyd George arranged for Christabel to receive £15,000[55] from the Treasury and private donors to fund her ongoing patriotic, anti-socialist campaigning and to encourage women to work in munitions factories.[56] Emmeline had already proven her own loyalty to Lloyd George by appearing at a wartime show trial of the socialist and former WSPU activist Alice Wheeldon and her daughters. These women were accused of plotting to kill the Prime Minister based on evidence cooked up by undercover officers and agents provocateurs. The Wheeldon family were anti-war activists who opened their home to men who fled conscription. Shortly before the Wheeldons were handed punitive sentences, Emmeline Pankhurst was unprecedentedly given the platform to speak from the witness box. She proceeded to praise Lloyd George effusively, insisting that these former WSPU members had nothing to do with her organisation and its patriotic cause.[57] By this time, Christabel and Emmeline were receiving cross-party praise for their wrecking abilities:

> Lloyd George remarked to the leader of the Conservatives, Andrew Bonar Law, in 1918, 'The Women's Party has been extremely useful … they have fought the Bolshevik and pacifist element with great skill, tenacity and courage.' Bonar Law evidently agreed, because when Christabel Pankhurst stood in the Smethwick constituency, he had the Conservative candidate withdraw, leaving Pankhurst to face only Labour.[58]

Male workers went on strike to oppose women working in munitions factories. This horrified Emmeline more for its lack of patriotism than for its sexism.[59] Christabel demanded iron rule in the factory, just as she did in the trenches: 'it is just the same in industry. There must be authority, control, discipline.'[60] Christabel and Emmeline both spoke out against wartime strikes and later opposed the 1926 General Strike.[61] Emmeline was to stand for Parliament as a Tory candidate but died in 1927 before a vote was cast. WSPU/Women's Party figures spoke in eugenic terms, linking the role of women to the propagation of the white race in service to nation and empire. Christabel argued, much as the WCTU did in America, and in notably fascistic language, that enfranchisement was necessary on the narrow, essentialist basis that white British women had 'a service to render, to the state as well as the home, to the race as well as the family.'[62] Sylvia noted that Christabel 'urged a working women's movement was of no value: working women were the weakest portion of the sex… Their lives were too hard, their education too meagre to equip them for the contest… [W]e want picked women, the very strongest and most intelligent!' In contrast, Sylvia's very first *Woman's Dreadnought* editorial, launched on International Women's Day in 1914, read: 'Some people say that the lives of working-women are too hard and their education too small for them to become a powerful force in winning the Vote, many though they are. Such people have forgotten their history.'[63]

As Emmeline and Christabel's horizons had narrowed, viewing votes for *some* women as an end in itself, a movement for itself, Sylvia's perspective only expanded. She saw the vote as a vital class *and* gender question that could open other paths to social justice. Her mother and sister insisted on equidistance from political parties – that the WSPU's quest relied on its 'neutrality.' Sylvia couldn't separate the fight against patriarchy from the class struggle and a workers movement from which much of the Pankhursts' politics had originated. Class division ripped through questions of citizenship and women's rights as constitutional reform neared and rights were bestowed by the state. The looser contours of the question of emancipation tightened as the question of *how* change would happen became polarised by assimilation questions – *in which order* should different groups be enfranchised? The WSPU demand was for woman suffrage on the basis of equality with men – a sleight of hand more likely to lead to equal voting rights for men and women of property, leaving most women and many working-class men still disenfranchised. Some suffragists genuinely cared about universal suffrage and working-class struggle, many didn't. Some labour movement men supported women's suffrage, others vehemently opposed it. The enmity between middle class women reformers and men of the workers movement, however, was increasingly challenged by the emergence of working class and socialist women who were also suffragists.[64] In 1918, all men and some propertied women over the age of 30 were added to the franchise. Interwar post-suffrage politics was a period of demobilisation and demoralisation for feminists. A national backlash in the 1920s attacked women voters and women politicians as ignorant and inferior. Broader unease festered about the country's demographic female majority, increased by the war's carnage. Women's employment, along with that of racialised workers, was blamed for (white) male unemployment. Another decade passed before all women over 21 got the vote. By then, Sylvia saw the struggle as being so much bigger: 'Women can no more put virtue into the decaying Parliamentary institution than can men: it is past reform and must disappear... The woman professional politician is neither more or less desirable than the man professional politician: the less the world has of either, the better.'[65]

The WSPU, like radical feminist and gender critical approaches, made the oppression of all women identical, while representing this identity through their own experiences, against which all other experiences were measured.[66] As Jules Joanne Gleeson and Elle O'Rourke write in their introduction to *Transgender Marxism*: 'What the earlier feminist movement had sought to destabilise now becomes anxiously reasserted.'[67] As they argue, 'here, the grit of trans women is abraded into the pearl of a rear-guard defence of female universalism.'[68] The story of the Pankhursts also mirrors the elitist, reactionary progressivism of Stanton and Anthony, if not for the dissident exception of Sylvia, who committed herself to workers emancipation and antiracism, organising alongside proletarian women, and Black and Jewish workers. While Sylvia and Christabel had their own divergent paths, the youngest Pankhurst sister, Adela, had the most extreme trajectory of all. She was disowned by her mother and emigrated to Australia where she was a founding member of the Communist Party in 1920. By 1941, she was a founding member of the fascist Australia First movement and named her dogs Adolf and Benito.[69] We can see across our case studies how during times of war, crisis and accelerated social change, the surging and collapsing of movement waves, people's political paths careened in unexpected ways.

We see this with contemporary gender critical feminists, some of whom began in left wing circles but an obsession with trans exclusion put them on a path to ideological flexibility on practically every other issue. Fast forward to 2023 and gender critical feminists are offering full-throated support for the British facilitation of Israel's genocide of the Palestinians. A month into the war, as Palestinians desperately turned to social media to document atrocities, Julie Bindel retweeted a *Telegraph* article by Alison Pearson, entitled, 'It's time to take a stand for civilisation.'[70] Much of the reaction from gender critical feminists was triggered by the participation of 'Sex Workers for a Free Palestine' and 'Queers for Palestine' in nationwide protests. Mary Harrington scoffed: 'a movement which has been likened to "Chickens for KFC"' before concluding with a defence of the US empire, 'with all its faults, America remains the principal guarantor of relative peace and order across a colossal sphere of influence that spans half the planet and includes my own nation.'[71] Gender critical feminism is a movement that has adapted variously and enthusiastically to 21st century national conservatism, imperialism and fascism. Just as Stanton and Anthony became more committed white supremacists and some reformers became Klanswomen, some Suffragettes became fascists, or simply imperialist Conservatives. What these passages in suffrage movements force us to recognise is that rebellion is not necessarily non-conformity.

4. The British Union of Fascists and Fascist Feminism?

A small number of ex-suffragettes sought the lost fellowship they remembered, as well as a promise of ultra-nationalist renewal, in the shape of Sir Oswald Mosley's British Union of Fascists which was founded in 1932. Though British women were enfranchised, suffrage movement veterans shared a sense of anti-climax. Many felt let down by the state and disillusioned by the next generation of women who inherited the rights *they* fiercely fought for. Canadian-born Mary Richardson had committed arson, bombed a railway station and, in 1914, hacked away at Velazquez's *Venus* painting at the National Gallery with a meat cleaver,[1] serving three years in prison – all for the suffragette cause. By the time she was middle aged, Richardson was active in the Independent Labour Party, standing as a Labour Party parliamentary candidate as late as 1931. Then she joined the BUF in 1933, citing its 'imperialism and action combined with discipline' as her reasons for joining.[2] Richardson was quickly promoted to the role of Chief Organiser of the BUF's Women's Section. She explained in 1934 that she 'was first attracted to the Blackshirts because [she] saw in them the courage, the action, the loyalty, the gift of service and the ability to serve which [she] had known in the suffragette movement.'[3] In reference to street battles the Mosleyites had with Communists and Jews, Richardson said: 'When later I discovered that Blackshirts were attacked for no visible cause or reason, I admired them the more when they hit back and hit back hard.'[4] The autonomy of the Women's Section, and its fortnightly paper *The Woman Fascist*, quickly waned and came under the tightening control of the party leadership. Having ascended to a position of power, and established a national club for fascist women, Richardson had also feuded with Oswald Mosley's mother, a powerful figure in the party. Richardson was expelled in 1935 for challenging the BUF's unequal pay structure.

Other former suffragettes also became fascists. Norah Elam and Mary Allen were close friends, sharing a passion for animal rights. The Irish-born Elam, a loyal lieutenant of the Pankhursts, who was made WSPU general secretary in 1913, was two decades later a trusted part of Mosley's inner circle and one of the BUF's many female election candidates.[5] Indeed, Elam was so trusted that Mosley transferred the party's funds into her name when it looked increasingly likely that he would be imprisoned. In fact, Elam was deemed important enough that the British state *also interned her* for over two years during World War Two, and so she returned to Holloway prison, a place she knew well from her suffragette days. Between her involvement in suffragism and fascism, Elam participated in anti-alien activism against Germans (and Jews) in Britain during World War One – calling in 1918 for the imprisonment of 'every man and woman of enemy blood, high and low, rich and poor.'[6] She was joined in this crusade by Emmeline and Christabel Pankhurst, as Simon Webb explains:

> It was the hope of the [Women's] party which [Christabel] and her mother formed in 1917 that Britain was to be for the British, that is to say ethnically homogenous. Both mother and daughter denied that it was possible for anybody to become a naturalized British subject. Christabel wanted to see naturalization certificates revoked. Another organizer of the WSPU who felt even more strongly on this subject was Norah [Elam]... In July 1918 [Elam] spoke at a rally in Trafalgar Square which was attended by 20,000 people who wished to see all Germans deported from Britain.[7]

Elam was also involved for much of her life in campaigning *for* vegetarianism and *against* vivisection and vaccination. She was a founding member of the London and Provincial Anti-Vivisection Society which by the mid-1930s was little more than a front organisation for the BUF.[8] In some of the first bourgeois animal rights groups of the late Victorian period, there were crossovers with the far right which can be traced to obsessions over kosher and halal forms of animal slaughter. This was the case for Norah Elam, as Webb explains:

> In reality, the traditional Jewish way of killing animals for food is no less humane than most methods and probably more so than some. There is no kind way of killing cows, sheep and chickens. Be that as it may, by the beginning of the twentieth century when Norah [Elam] helped set up the London and Provincial Anti-Vivisection Society, the genuine concern for the welfare of helpless animals often became bound up in this way with a dislike and mistrust of Jews. This was happening in other countries besides Britain. In Germany, anxiety about the welfare of animals generally, and the practice of kosher slaughter in particular, were features of right-wing and anti-Semitic groups at the end of the nineteenth century. Such views found favour with the nascent National Socialist Party in the 1920s. Hitler was famously a vegetarian and great lover of animals and one of the first things which the Nazis did on coming to power in 1933 was 'to ban kosher slaughter and outlaw vivisection.'[9]

Suffragette fascists

Elam, like Richardson, linked her fascism to her time as a suffragette, calling it the 'logical, if much grander, conception of the momentous issues raised by the militant women of a generation ago.'[10] She was a prominent speaker and writer for the BUF. In February 1935, Elam wrote in *The Blackshirt*:

> No woman who loves her country, her sex or her liberty, need fear the coming victory of fascism. Rather, she will find what the suffragettes dreamt about twenty odd years ago is now becoming a possibility, and woman will buckle on her armour for the last phase of the greatest struggle, for the liberation of the human race, which the world has yet seen.[11]

Elam's granddaughter and great-granddaughter have written that her

> Articles give a clue to the way in which Mosley made use of her to counter anti-fascist claims: 'Fascism will Mean Real Equality'; 'J'Accuse – Failure of the Women's Movement'; 'Women, Fascism and Democracy'. The common themes in [Elam's] articles are trenchant criticism of the failure of women to make any headway within the democratic party political system. [Elam] frequently pointed out that having been a suffragette, she had a greater authority to pronounce on these issues than others.[12]

Elam's fascism was unrepentant until her death in 1961. Her antisemitism was long held and vicious; she even sent her 12-year-old son to live in Germany in 1934 so that he could join the Hitler Youth.[13]

Mary Sophia Allen left her conservative, wealthy family as a young woman to join the WSPU, later becoming a paid organiser. She committed multiple arson attacks and was imprisoned and force-fed more than once. Allen was tasked with the important job of organising and stewarding Emily Davison's funeral after she famously threw herself in front of the King's horse at the Epsom Derby and martyred herself for the suffragette cause. Following her suffragism, Allen and her lover, Margaret Damer Dawson, became pioneers of women's policing. This was a vocation that Allen and several other former suffragettes pursued for many years. Believing strongly in the importance of women's representation in policing, Dawson and Allen were particularly interested in policing the morality of working class women.[14] Dawson had earlier split from a wartime volunteer police force she co-organised with Nina Boyle because Boyle, a feminist and suffragist, worried about what impact the extraordinary powers of the wartime Defence of the Realm Act (DORA) would have on the policing of women's public conduct, fearing a return to the Contagious Diseases Act of the previous century. Dawson and Allen had no such qualms, they were positively motivated in their mission to crack down on 'vice', prostitution and 'white slavery', to enforce the correct behaviour of women of the lower orders. Allen was awarded an OBE for her wartime efforts in 1918. The authorities withdrew their support for Allen and her recruits after the war but she continued to dress in uniform and present herself as a serving officer, becoming a nuisance to the Metropolitan Police. In the 1920s, Allen's attraction to authoritarianism became more formally aligned with fascism and a passionate anti-communism. She organised a new volunteer police force, the Women's Auxiliary Service,[15] during the 1926 General Strike which she believed nothing less than the trade unions seeing 'an appropriate occasion on which to put a pistol to the head of England, and demand her surrender to a Communist coup.'[16] Allen broadcast an appeal for volunteers (that is, strikebreakers) on the newly inaugurated BBC and 'thousands of women came forward to help'[17] with 'Two aeroplanes, nearly two hundred cars, hospitality, sleeping accommodation, and several complete houses ... put at our disposal.'[18] Her volunteer force would be supplemented by Lucy Baldwin, the wife of the Tory Prime Minister, and by Allen's old leader, Emmeline Pankhurst.[19]

Allen would take her obsession with uniformed women's policing into an unsuccessful political candidacy, standing as an MP in 1922 under the slogan: 'Mary Allen, who knows where she is.'[20] She set out to spread the good word about women's policing capabilities in multiple tours around the world – this included meetings with Hitler and Franco, as well as helping to institute women's policing regimes in British colonies like Ireland, Egypt and Palestine. She maintained close contacts with senior Nazi leaders for many years and was head of the BUF's Women's Section in the late 1930s. By then she had been part of several British far right groups for over a decade. Known by everyone simply as 'The Commandant', Allen always dressed in uniform and had shortly cropped hair. She tried to launch another women's militia in 1933, the Women's Reserve, which resembled an 'anti-communist, paramilitary force.'[21] As Julie V. Gottlieb put it, 'Allen's road to fascism was logically sign-posted, and the progress from women in blue to women in black was not a grand leap.'[22] Though the British state opted not to intern Allen, she was essentially put under house arrest. She remained faithful to Mosley's failed postwar attempts to revive his movement and stayed friends with Norah Elam until her death. Mary Allen largely withdrew from public life from the 1950s onwards, other than her role as a judge at Crufts.[23]

Other connections between British suffragism and the interwar far right include the leading WSPU member, Flora Drummond, who also led women against strikers in the 1926 General Strike.[24] Drummond formed the Women's Guild of Empire in 1928, an anti-Communist group. Mercedes Barrington, a suffragette, later joined the BUF and stood as a parliamentary candidate.[25] Lady Houston, one of the WSPU's biggest donors, operated in British far right circles for the remainder of her life.[26] Women's involvement in the far right was not new by this point, after all.

The first explicitly fascist group in Britain, the British Fascisti, later renamed the British Fascists (BF), was set up by Rotha Lintorn-Orman in 1923, a young queer woman from a wealthy military family who was driven by a vitriolic anti-communism.[27] The group had a large number of women members and developed women's units with special women's patrols and children's clubs. In 1925, the assistant director of the BF's women's units claimed: 'We want to get a great scheme of social work going all over the country... [W]e want to make our Fascist badge known everywhere, as something that stands for practical good and practical help then you'll find there won't be much Communism in the country.'[28] The British Fascists never grew to meet those ambitions but it had close links to the Conservative Party, to military top brass, to MI5, to members of the aristocracy and to other fascist groups that formed through splits from the BF. Dowager Viscountess Dorothy Downe was an enthusiastic supporter of both the British Fascists and later the BUF, only avoiding wartime internment because she was King George V's goddaughter.[29] Nesta Webster was also a member of the BF and the BUF, among other far right groups. She had garnered a public profile through her writings about the Illuminati, the Freemasons and Judeo-Bolshevik conspiracies. Her writings on the latter were later praised by Winston Churchill.[30] Webster contributed to the notorious 1920 'Jewish Peril' series in the *Morning Post* (which became *The Daily Telegraph* in 1937), centring around the forged *Protocols of the Learned Elders of Zion*. The series was later published as a book called *The Cause of World Unrest*.

Living a no less noble life

Women made up around a quarter of the British Union of Fascist's membership overall. The size and class composition of the membership fluctuated greatly over the course of the party's existence as its policies, favourability in press coverage and political fortunes waxed and waned. It attracted working class women members in the East End of London and in the depressed manufacturing regions of Lancashire. It had thriving branches in Newcastle, Sussex and Belfast. Middle class and petit bourgeois recruits, housewives and teachers, predominated but upper class and aristocratic members and supporters were key to the party's existence and leadership. All kinds of women became members. The silent movie star Joan Morgan joined the BUF, blaming Jews for the decline of Britain's film industry. The internationally famous Irish motorcyclist Fay Taylour was also a committed member and was interned during the war. TS Eliot's first wife, Vivienne Haigh-Wood, was briefly a member. Young aristocrat Unity Mitford was infamously a proud Blackshirt. She was a younger sister of Oswald Mosley's second wife, Diana, both of them cousins of Winston Churchill. Unity was a Nazi from a young age, even becoming a close companion of Adolf Hitler through her regular visits to Germany. Dorothy 'Dotty' Clark, an actress and the daughter of a WSPU suffragette, took a similar political journey to that of Adela Pankhurst. She was in the Independent Labour Party for many years and was a Communist sympathiser until the mid-1930s. Then, following a visit to Germany, where she was introduced to Hitler by Unity Mitford, she became a passionate Nazi. Her second husband, Peter Eckersley, a cousin of the novelist Aldous Huxley, was a radio engineer and one of the key figures in the founding of the BBC in the 1920s. Peter became a close associate of Mosley and joined the BUF, while Dorothy was a member of a smaller but even more explicitly Nazi grouping – Arnold Leese's Imperial Fascist League. Dorothy ended up defecting to Nazi Germany, working on wartime propaganda for the Third Reich's English-language radio broadcasts into England and recruiting William Joyce (another former BUF member) into becoming 'Lord Haw Haw.'

Over the mid-1930s, BUF women (and men) became ever more devoted to Oswald Mosley's leadership cult as the party further embraced national socialism. BUF women were just as racist as their male counterparts. Indeed, virulent antisemitism was regularly synthesised through discourses on women's issues. White British women were seen as being the most vulnerable to a specifically Jewish poisoning of the national culture, with its corruption of family values and the dilution of Britain's racial stock. Julie V. Gottlieb quotes one female BUF member, asking:

> The instability of our homes, the pseudo-scientific study called psycho-analysis, the discontents occasioned in British families by the falsity of Hollywood sex-filled entertainment, the pernicious doctrine of Marxism, the destruction of the family by use of contraceptives: can it be seriously denied that all these things have originated from the Jew?[31]

Gottlieb explains that 'Anti-Semitism was always reinforced by arousing anxieties about sexual potency, and women were portrayed as the symbolic victims of a Jew-ravaged Britain.'[32] The figure of the predatory Jewish man, like the one mobilised by the 1920s Klan in the US, was depicted as an unscrupulous employer of British women, a demonic perpetrator of assaults and sex traffic, or a purveyor of pornography. Eileen Lyons, a BUF member and a frequent writer in party publications, illustrated this vision of Jewish exploiters[33] and totalising Jewish control:

> One may be an ardent Tory, Socialist, or even Liberal, but is it going to get 'Our Mary' out of the Jewish sweat-shop? Is it going to make the old Jew pay decent wages? No! Is not Financial Democracy afraid of the Rosenbaums, or perhaps it would be truer to say are not the Rosenbaums Financial Democracy?[34]

Sweated labour, vice and 'white slave traffic' – discourses around which had long been thoroughly racialised as Jewish exploits in Britain – had also been campaigning issues for the suffragettes. And this type of antisemitism was equally present in the writing and speeches of some leading suffragettes before and during World War One. During the 'Marconi Scandal' of 1912 – a government corruption scandal that due to some of the characters involved being Jewish became cause for an antisemitic moral panic – Flora Drummond of the WSPU said:

> The Jews were dominating the country in the persons of Sir Rufus Isaacs and Mr Herbert Samuel, and the women now emphatically protested against these dictators making their laws. If they were English it would not so much matter, but they were not. This was one of the principle reasons that women wanted the vote.[35]

Christabel Pankhurst also leaned into antisemitic conspiracy theory to construct her worldview, as Simon Webb makes clear:

> On 10 July 1917, Christabel Pankhurst gave a speech which was reported in great detail in the 13 July edition of *Britannia*. In it, she outlined her view that German Jews controlled the course of world history and that through 'international finance', German-Jewish bankers were able to attack British interests. A few quotations should be sufficient to give a flavour of the thing. She began by telling the audience at the Aeolian Hall in London that Britain faced two enemies. One was the alliance of avowedly enemy nations, consisting of Germany, Austria-Hungary, Bulgaria and Turkey. The second was 'International Finance'.[36]

The BUF produced extensive policy, speeches, publications and propaganda outlining their vision for the role of women, of family structure and of sexual propriety not only in the party but in a future fascist Britain. There was a clear gender hierarchy and an essentialist ideology determining women and men's 'natural' roles and strengths. The party saw women's work as being generally limited to caring and nurturing jobs like teaching and midwifery. If women were to be leaders in a fascist Britain, it would only be to lead other women. The BUF vision was of a highly developed modern economy with full employment of the male citizenry and a 'family wage' sufficient to keep most women in the domestic sphere. The BUF sought to politicise this sphere – to emphasise, rather than invisibilise, domestic work, claiming it represented women's value to the state and to fascist life. The ideal for womanhood was to be 'mothers of the race' and wombs for the state. As Mosley put it in his manifesto, *The Greater Britain*, 'we want men who are men and women who are women.'[37] A 1934 article in *The Blackshirt* similarly proclaimed: 'Fascism sees women as complementary and equal to man, standing beside him in no less honourable a fight, living a no less noble life, achieving in domesticity things parallel and of equal importance with man.'[38] The conformist environment of the BUF presumed the heterosexuality of its membership (despite many gay male BUF members)[39] and set clear expectations for the way that women were expected to look and act. Fascists, including fascist women, attacked their enemies for not conforming to these standards of gender presentation and behaviour. 'Fascist women,' writes Gottlieb,

> Maligned Modernism, Bloomsbury, Bright Young Things, spinsters, mannish-women, the 'Red' woman who gave them trouble when stewarding meetings, and attempted to warn their female counterparts about the corrupting influences of women's magazines and cinema-going. Their attacks were most frequently gibes at the opponents' physical attributes or presumed sexual orientation.[40]

Such discourses were able to survive exceptions and contradictions, like Mary Allen, for example, who was a lesbian, gender non-conforming in appearance and was known to her friends as Robert.[41]

The BUF liked to play up its claims to inheriting the suffragette tradition, publicising its former suffragettes as strong militant women, even if fascism promised to do away with liberal democracy and voting rights entirely. The legacy of the suffragettes – and the defining of feminism – became battlegrounds, fought over by veterans of the movement who had since scattered themselves across the political spectrum. The international socialism of Sylvia Pankhurst, the conservative imperialism of her mother and sister and the fascism of BUF women all laid claim to the legacy of a movement based on women's autonomy, self-activity and direct action to force a change in women's legal and political status that, once enacted, they were sure would not be reversed. Each suffragette-turned-fascist had first sought integration into an existing system that they had put their bodies on the line to oppose. Each stood unsuccessfully for a main party: Mary Richardson for Labour, Mary Allen for the Liberals and Norah Elam for the Tories. Their leader, Mosley, himself exemplified the slipperiness of party-political affiliation during the turbulence of the interwar period. An aristocratic former Conservative MP turned proto-Keynesian employment minister in Ramsay MacDonald's Labour government, Sir Oswald Mosley quickly moved on from his failed venture, the New Party, to launch what became the largest fascist party in British history.

Disillusioned progressives

In some ways, the resentful, racist lashing out following personal and political defeats of Richardson, Allen and Elam are comparable to Stanton and Anthony's following the disintegration of the AERA. Gottlieb writes,

> Each believed that she was owed more than she had received for her dedication to the women's suffrage struggle, and that

this inheritance had remained wanting. In their ultimate rejection of liberal democracy, each in her political life personified the disillusionment and the disappointed hopes of politicised women in post-suffrage Britain.[42]

A similar personal trajectory can be found on Britain's far right today. Anne Marie Waters founded the now defunct far right 'For Britain' party following her lost leadership campaign in UKIP. A Dublin-born lesbian, Waters is reminiscent of the fascist suffragettes in that she twice unsuccessfully sought selection as a Labour parliamentary candidate before her turn towards a more hardened Islamophobic politics. In 2023 Waters rejoined UKIP and released a snippet of a chapter of her forthcoming book, *Women Erased*, on her Substack, in which she defends Emmeline Pankhurst from being cancelled today by Black Lives Matter.[43] Similarly, the BUF ex-suffragettes were scathing about the political paths taken by other suffragists following enfranchisement, and yet 'in some sense … still regarded themselves as feminists.'[44] They continued to identify with the suffragette legacy, believing that women should be active in politics. In a 1936 article in the BUF journal *Action*, Norah Elam explained how she saw enfranchised women being incorporated into all of the existing political parties and saw the entire system as being under the control of 'wirepullers' and influential Jewish men:

> Seeing that party women once again wear the primrose in the memory of the Jew Disraeli, the rosette in honour of Sir Herbert Samuel, the red emblem in commemoration of Karl Marx; they have turned again as handmaidens to the hewing of wood and drawing of water for the party wirepullers, and they add to all this futility the cross upon the ballot paper once in every five years.[45]

It is interesting too to note Elam's use of the term "handmaiden" to describe women who she believed were being duped by the system. The same word is used today, taken from Margaret Atwood's 1985 novel *The Handmaid's Tale*, by gender critical activists to derogate cisgender women who stand in solidarity with their trans sisters.[46]

While BUF policy was undoubtedly constructed by male leaders, it would be wrong to reduce party women to downtrodden bystanders. It would also be wrong to assume that they were any less passionate in their fascist beliefs compared to their male comrades. When BUF women led large meetings in 1939, calling for peace with Nazi Germany in what they rejected as a 'Jewish War', the *Jewish Chronicle*, using decidedly sexist language, reported that the women 'adopted a more hysterical anti-Jewish attitude than did their men-folk.'[47] BUF women took part in most party activities: marching, stewarding, public speaking, fundraising, selling newspapers, fighting. There was a Women's Defence Force, trained in jiu-jitsu – as were the suffragettes before them – and involved in constant street battles with Jews and communists. BUF women stood for election. Like the WKKK, BUF women played a key role in recruiting new members. Come election time, they presented a softer face of fascism. The party publication, *The Fascist Week*, explained: 'Fascism in Britain knows that its women members go a long way to help the cause; and that it is a woman's influence that has converted many male members.' Gottlieb agrees:

> The feminine presence on the door-steps of the nation went some way towards disarming public apprehensions of BUF hooliganism and disorderliness... [W]omen were to act as the publicists, the temptresses, and the vendors of fascism to a British market suspicious of fascism's machismo and masculine aggression.[48]

The BUF proudly trumpeted its higher percentage of women candidates than other parties. Oswald Mosley often referred to those who he sought the support of as 'normal women,' capturing something of the gender critical reliance today on what Bassi and LaFleur in *Transgender Studies Quarterly* call a 'feminism of the 99%.' That is, the 'idea that what should ... bring women together is a shared self-definition as biologically overdetermined and authentically gendered subjects.'[49] Mosley said:

> We are pledged to complete sex equality. The German attitude towards women has always been different from the British, and my movement has been largely built up by the fanaticism of women; they hold ideals with tremendous passion. Without the women I could not have got a quarter of the way.[50]

An even greater dependence on BUF women came in later years as so many male Blackshirts were either drafted or imprisoned. Women members took the lead in the party's 'peace campaign' – a front for recruitment and an attempt to demoralise a national effort for war which the BUF opposed. The British state proscribed the party in 1940. Its leading members were interned, including well over a hundred women. Some of them rejoined Mosley's postwar fascist effort, the Union Movement, set up in 1948.

As with the Women of the Ku Klux Klan, a party politics of everyday life had developed through the growth of the British Union of Fascists. Party structures helped to cement gender roles and harden racial hatred. BUF weddings were held as happy couples consecrated their vows before party and leader. While the KKK bonded through their enjoyment of blackface minstrelsy, the BUF had 'Jazz Without Jews' played by the 'Aryan Dance Band.'[51] In keeping with past white women's movements, women 'of the race' were seen as the guardians of morality and respectability. BUF women led the party's opposition to pornography, prostitution, loose morals and sexual perversion. The party saw in Britain a corrupted national state, what they referred to as a decadent 'financial democracy,' which they attributed to Jewish control.

The family unit was the domain of the fascist woman. It stood as a microcosm of the perfectible fascist corporate state. White British women, at the height of imperium, were to British fascism the 'gatekeepers of the national community'[52] – key to the survival of the race. Fascist women were also enlisted in a priority struggle for the fascist project: the flourishing of a warrior society and the regeneration of a British masculinity – seen, as by the far right today, to have been emasculated by feminism. Like the second Ku Klux Klan, BUF ideology denied the importance of class division. Gendered division was natural and welcomed and unity was to be found in racial purity and service to nation and state.

Defining fascist feminism?

These comparative historical scenes intend to draw out some problems with how we define fascism and indeed ask whether definitional debates are adequate to the problem at hand. Asking whether definitions of fascism are adequate is commonplace, but in the case of fascist feminism the issue of definition is thornier still. We began this book with Asa Seresin's provocation in conversation with Sophie Lewis, which is worth repeating as we near its conclusion. 'What if certain forms of feminism, historically, have not simply colluded with white-supremacist projects but have actually been fascist themselves?' Seresin asks this because, in her view, anti-fascism might be strengthened by 'ceasing to deny' that this was the case. What do we gain from asserting this hypothesis and what risks are there of doing so? What organisational questions arise from it? Historian Julie V. Gottlieb has proved an important consultant in this regard, as her monograph, *Feminine Fascism*, which we have greatly leant on in this chapter, made the problem of women and fascism central to understanding the BUF. Her thesis also formed part of the dialogue between Sophie Lewis and Asa Seresin, who reminds us:

> Historians who work on the role of women in fascist movements often express surprise that women would be invested in a political ideology that is inherently anti-feminist and misogynistic. Yet female fascists themselves expressed a strong belief that fascism had something to offer women, and I don't think we should rush to dismiss this as false consciousness. Fascism did have much to offer certain subsets of white

women who were invested in upholding white supremacy as well as conservative social norms surrounding the family, religious morality, and social purity.[53]

We might expect Gottlieb to be a historian who makes this connection, but in fact she argues, 'no such doctrinal position as fascist feminism, was, or is, possible.'[54] Unlike Blee and MacLean, as well as other feminist historians of fascism, Gottlieb denies the connection, even as she describes a transition of feminists to anti-feminist politics. In another passage, however, she seems to contradict herself: 'perhaps the development of the fascist feminist type can tell us as much about the potential of Edwardian radical feminism as about the nature of the BUF's women's policy.'[55] As Gottlieb's historical research helps to shape much of the argument of this chapter and continues to inform current debates on gender critical feminism, it is worth exploring this ambiguity more carefully. Is fascist feminism *possible*, or not? Is this term period specific and limited to describing an Edwardian transition from suffrage and suffragette activism to fascism? Or does feminism have a conceptual relation to fascism that is recursive, as Lewis and Seresin seem to suggest? Attempting to answer these questions will help us clarify our own stance on fascist feminism as both a historiographical issue and an anti-fascist organisational question.

The sticking point here is how feminism is defined. Gottlieb asks: 'is not one of the tests of a commitment to the equality of the sexes the acceptance of liberal democratic principles?'[56] Lintorn-Orman, leader of British Fascisti, is given as an example. Barbara Storm Farr used the term fascist feminist[57] to describe Lintorn-Orman and this Gottlieb rejects: 'in claiming Lintorn-Orman for women's history, and even for the history of interwar feminism, Farr prolongs the tradition of the revision of British fascist leaders inaugurated by Robert Skidelsky in his 1975 biography of Sir Oswald Mosley.'[58] If we put to one side the question of revisionism, the description of Lintorn-Orman given by Farr (and cited by Gottlieb) is hardly inaccurate: 'a unique expression of an activist right-wing woman who discarded traditional female roles and attempted to build a hierarchical para-military organization among the middle and upper-middle levels of society.'[59] However, Gottlieb argues that Lintorn-Orman is not a fascist feminist because as a fascist she was no longer a liberal feminist: 'there was no room for women's rights in her political conceptions.'[60]

However, by this same measure, the liberal feminist tradition could also be called anti-feminist, or at the very least, be understood as a specific form of racialised anti-feminism. This is where the broader circumstances of the society that assembles fascism become as important as the fascist phenomena itself. Moral equality, the liberal democratic principle that organised early feminist movements, was only ever a contingent equality. As we have shown, from the very beginning, white feminists within the liberal tradition abstracted the women's question from the perspectives and struggles of proletarian, racialised, indigenous and other colonised women. The early feminist tradition was anti-woman from the perspectives of marginalised (ie, the majority of) women. This abstraction of the women's question as white continued to recur through each new feminist wave. Many Black women in the 1960s and 70s, and beyond, have been sceptical of the term feminist for precisely this reason. See an account of a member of the Brixton Black Women's Group, founded in 1973: 'We would not have called ourselves "feminists" by any means – we didn't go that far for many years. It took us a long time before we worked out a Black women's perspective, which took account of race, class, sex, and sexuality.'[61] Winifred Breines writes, 'Many black women were reluctant to consider themselves feminists in part, of course, because of its association with white feminism and the fear that it would split the black community.'[62]

The liberal democratic tradition is most definitely contestable as a foundation for women's equality. Gottlieb is reluctant to let go of positive identifications with liberal democratic principles, and this also manifests in an inadequate historicisation of race and racism. As she writes, 'the real question, of course, is whether there could be a place for any discourse of rights in an anti-alien, anti-Semitic ideology? How can such a discourse [feminism] be integrated within one which focuses on the denial of citizenship rights to others?'[63] As a counterpoint, we struggle to find examples from the political cultures of the British Edwardian era through to the 1930s where the discourse of rights was not the means to pursue a violent exclusionary politics. Prime Minister Arthur Balfour was anti-alien and antisemitic, passing the 1905 Aliens Act, Britain's first modern immigration controls, which targeted Jewish workers and refugees. In 1917, as Foreign Secretary, he signed the declaration that bears his name, stating that the Jews he wanted out of Britain had a right to Palestinian land. James Renton, in his chapter in the volume *The Jew as Legitimation*, argues that British imperial race-thinking, including its racist belief in conspiratorial Jewish Power, was central to its support for Zionism. Part of an attempt to curry favour for its war effort,

> Foreign Secretary Balfour, Lloyd George and other senior British policy-makers believed that Jewish power could be a significant weapon in the struggle to meet these challenges. Convinced of enemy influence among US Jewry and of heavy Jewish involvement in antiwar and radical circles in Russia, the Foreign Office and the War Cabinet wished to channel Jewish power in favor of Britain and its allies. With their racial nationalist conception of ethnicity, they became convinced that Zionism was the best means of achieving this ambition. Balfour summarized this logic for the cabinet at the meeting that approved the declaration that was to bear his name, on 31 October: 'The vast majority of Jews in Russia and America, as, indeed, all over the world, now appeared to be favourable to Zionism. If we could make a declaration favourable to such an ideal, we should be able to carry on extremely useful propaganda both in Russia and America.'[64]

In the same period that Rotha Lintorn-Orman grew her racist organisation, the British Fascisti, many within the labour movement lobbied parliament to deny the right of citizenship to Jews, who were racialised fellow workers. Indeed, racism was a pre-condition to nationalise labour rights and therefore secure a popular conception of whiteness for the British working class. Anti-immigration sentiment and action underpinned temperance and suffrage causes in Britain and the US, as we have argued. In no period of racial capitalism have rights been gained without removing the rights of others. Indeed, rights are often secured through the exclusion of *the other*.[65]

Let's now return to how Gottlieb frames her investigation into the BUF feminisation of fascism specifically: 'Claiming to represent *true feminism* by recognizing the irreversibility of women's emancipation, the BUF's feminine fascism applauded those aggressive aspects of women's activism essential to the success of a nascent fascist movement.'[66] Gottlieb is concerned with the incorporation of progressive era feminist militancy into fascism, which we agree is central, as it is in the case of the WKKK. The unique political experience that women brought to fascism is the most important historical consideration. However, Gottlieb also argues that women drifted to fascism because communism failed to mobilise their political skills and experience. Seresin challenges this argument, however, writing:

> There is an interesting moment in Julie Gottlieb's *Feminine Fascism* where she blames communist class reductionism for 'stunting the development' of feminist antifascism. I think this does an injustice to the long tradition of feminist antifascism while simultaneously scapegoating communist movements for the fact that some women were drawn to fascism.[67]

It is true that Gottlieb seems too keen to make this argument. A quote from the *Journal of the Women's Commission of the Spartacist League* in 1981 is held up as representative of 'attitudes' that 'can be traced back to the inter-war period.'[68] Yet this abstracts from British feminist communists of the inter-war period. Sylvia Pankhurst's renaming of the *Woman's Dreadnought* to the *Workers' Dreadnought* provides the obvious counterpoint to this assumption. Both her family in the suffrage movement and her

lovers within the socialist movement had all failed to accommodate her revolutionary positions. Sylvia's view on feminism
was not, however, stunted by class analysis. Her feminist viewpoint was *clarified* by a revolutionary transition into what we
would now recognise as a form of anti-colonial revolutionary
communist feminism. Feminism not only survives the interwar
transition, then, but ideological strands within the early feminist
current *are developed and sharpened*. We can also see this happen
for Mary Richardson and Norah Elam in a different ideological
register. Indeed, far from withdrawing from liberal democratic
principles, Elam found her transition to fascism more straightforward because those principles were already prepared for her
as an advocate of the liberal tradition. This is clear in the way
Elam registers her ongoing loyalty to the work of John Stuart
Mill – a state philosopher and indeed 'state feminist' that aligned
with much early reform and social purity-based campaigning of
the 1870s, as explored in the chapter prior to this. Elam, once a
suffragette, then a fascist, wrote in 1935:

> Every student of politics realizes that the issue now lies be-
> tween Fascism and Communism. So far as British women are
> concerned, Communism makes little appeal. To go no fur-
> ther, it is the philosophy of destruction, and is the negation
> of the natural instincts of womanhood. It is the antithesis
> of every principle and practice which women value and re-
> quire.[69]

Elam is clear that communism has 'little appeal' because it is 'the
antithesis of every principle ... which women value and require',
but what are these principles? Elam continues,

> Fascism seems to be the only solution. It has within it every
> principle peculiarly suitable and adaptable to the genius of
> the British character. It offers real freedom and liberty to all
> men and women of goodwill towards this country. Lest there
> should be any misunderstanding, we shall define these so
> often loosely-used terms, in words with which no democrat

will quarrel, for they are taken from that apostle of unadulterated democracy, John Stuart Mill.

'The sole end,' he wrote, 'for which mankind are warranted individually or collectively in interfering with the liberty of action of any of their number, is self-protection. The only purpose for which power can be rightfully exercised over any member of a civilized community against his will is to prevent harm to others.'

This is precisely the Fascist conception of individual liberty, and it is obviously a conception that so far as women are concerned gives them every opportunity that they can legitimately require in their future status as women citizens. In no other system are these principles embodied.[70]

We do not need to take fascists at their word to register the historical conductivity of liberal authoritarianism, which is contained within the ingenious flexibility of Mill's 'harm principle', and the 'fascist solution' Elam attaches to it. Interestingly, Mill contradicted his principle when he opposed the Contagious Diseases Acts because he argued this intrusion of the state on the individual liberty of women was not legitimate. The purity feminist movements that emerged to police working-class women to protect them from harms were in fact more militant advocates of this reasoning. In 1935 Elam found in Mill a fascist solution. Not only is fascist feminism possible, then, but according to Elam, the promise of fascist feminism is 'precisely' liberal. We could be even more upfront and say that the transition from liberal feminism to fascist feminism was not only possible, for some *it was easy*. Withdrawing from the liberal feminist tradition in order to redefine the egalitarian breadth of feminism was *much harder*. 'Ironically,' Gottlieb writes, 'one way in which British fascist women proved their agency and independence was by giving free reign to their own racial hatreds.'[71] But was this so different to how many early feminists progressed their feminism? When we look at the positions taken by Elizabeth Cady Stanton and

Susan B. Anthony or by Christabel and Emmeline Pankhurst, we can see how easily their arguments could have appeared in the propaganda of the WKKK or the BUF. It was not such a great leap to move from a natural affinity with the nation and the white race to an embrace of fascism. Sylvia was not the only one but, as an anti-colonial communist, she was an outlier in the British left, never mind the women's movement. Both Christabel and Emmeline had turned solidly towards imperialism by 1914. Sylvia Pankhurst's proximity to the Irish anti-colonial struggle, East End mutual aid movements and Black internationalism compelled her complete withdrawal from the liberal feminist tradition and an embrace of class struggle that was ranging and empirically situated.

Implications for anti-fascism?

Due to a rise in far right and fascist causes in the 21st century that promote pro-natalist themes (and are often led by women), feminist historians have begun to revise historiographies of feminism and fascism. While we can only touch on the matter here, we are interested in how the relationship between fascism and the women's cause, when applied to different circumstances, challenges general explanations for why fascism could appeal to women. Part of the hypothesis given by Gottlieb is that an economistic Marxist position failed to draw women into anti-fascist movements and resulted in fascists recruiting women into their own organisations. This fails to address the peculiar circumstances of ideological fracture and drift within the British-Irish women's cause. In addition, this 'fascist-Marxist' opposition, which prevails in Marxist theories of fascism as well, can fail to appreciate the various circumstances of social struggle in interwar Europe. The battle between fascism and communism and anarchist forces in interwar Europe is central to understanding the interwar histories of Germany, Spain and Italy. However, the racial, colonial and religious assembling of a fascist cause in these countries was also varied and this must impact on how the women's question is studied. What about Ireland, the birthplace of Elam? The Proclamation of the Irish Republic, issued during the Easter Rising in 1916, was one of the most far reaching and progressive statements on women's equality of the period.[72] However, the divisive instrument that set off the Irish civil war (1922-) and ultimately brought the Irish revolutionary period to a close was the Anglo-Irish Treaty of 1921, drafted by Winston Churchill to incite division within the republican forces. What became known as the 'Treaty split' between 'pro-Treaty' and 'anti-Treaty' forces provides yet another example of the barbarism of a liberal peace. It is also a moment of significant fracture within the Irish women's cause and a plausible site of a fascist or proto-fascist feminist transition.

Hanna Sheehy-Skeffington, who we briefly mention in the last chapter when recounting the British-Irish suffragette split, supported the anti-Treaty IRA in 1922 along with many other Irish feminists during the civil war. In a letter to US suffragist Alice Park, she writes, 'the treaty is a bad compromise and I fear we are in for some decades of reaction under a temporary false prosperity, reinforced by our native militarism!'[73] Throughout her time in the IWFL and beyond, Sheehy-Skeffington was anti-war and a pacifist. She also supported the use of arms where there was an opportunity to 'be freed for ever from British rule by a swift uprising', while remaining radically opposed to 'War and Militarism'.[74] Again, the militancy of suffragist women, as well as the parting of ways of women through the specific imperial stresses of the period, is what stands out in Ireland. We need only compare Elam's trajectory[75] with Skeffington's and that of Margaret Skinnider, as related by her Irish feminist biographer, Mary McAuliffe,

> She was this young Scottish woman ... one of the few women who actually participated in military action during 1916. She could shoot. She was a trained markswoman; wounded three times, was operated on by the first-aid women in the College of Surgeons. Miraculously survived. Then the other thing you would hear about her is she applied for a pension in the early 1920s and was refused because the government said

that the pension, the military pension was for soldiers, which is recognised only in the masculine sense. And that was it. That's all I ever knew of Margaret Skinnider. Luckily, Margaret had written an eyewitness account of 1916 in 1917, and then of course I discovered that she was actually one of the women who went to America, 1917, 1918, with Hanna Sheehy Skeffington and Nellie Gifford and Min Ryan, and many of the other women who were also out in 1916 giving information to the Irish-American public about what they said was the true story of the Rising in Ireland. And I just have it here and she says here in the first chapter, she says, 'My father and mother are Irish, but had lived almost all their lives in Scotland, and much of the time in Glasgow. She says Scotland is my home, but Ireland is my country. And she talked about the fact that they used to come back to Monaghan.' So the Skinniders are originally from Monaghan. She began to read history books and she was very impacted about the story of the famine and the inequalities in Ireland and the land war and all of those things, that history of dispossession and colonization, immigration, forced immigration and all that, that her peoples, Irish people, went through. But also, she's growing up in Glasgow and Glasgow is a very interesting place at this time, particularly for working-class communities. And it's really known as, you know, there's a lot of radical socialist thinking, particularly among working-class areas in Clydeside, it was known as Red Clydeside. There's a lot of militant feminist activism. She's also immediately by 1913/14 … joining the Irish volunteers in Glasgow firstly and then Cumann na mBan when it's set up. From about late 1914 onwards, she is involved in attempted raids on shipbuilding industries in Glasgow to get gelignite and arms and ammunition for the Irish volunteers in Ireland.[76]

Skinnider defied gendered expectations of women at the time and was in a relationship with a fellow Cumann na mBan fighter, Nora O'Keeffe. Many historians have argued that feminist militancy in anti-colonial Ireland included independent fighting units and was far more radically integrated into revolutionary struggles than in Britain, the US and throughout Europe.[77] Indeed, McAuliffe has shown that during the civil war, pro-Treaty forces, led by men, targeted radical Cumann na mBan women in Kerry and used sexual abuse as a weapon of war due to the threat they posed to pro-Treaty forces. McAuliffe writes, 'The militancy of anti-Treaty Cumann na mBan, the support of its members for the anti-Treaty forces, and especially their contribution to anti-Treaty propaganda campaigns made them dangerous opponents that the Free State and its army needed to contain and control.'[78] Many pro-Treaty women also targeted anti-Treaty women with punitive and violent reprisals for resistance, setting off a cycle of reprisals between former comrades.[79] In recent writing on the Blue Blouses, the women's regiment of the Blueshirts, an anti-republican, anti-communist 1930s offshoot of the pro-Treaty women's movements, McAuliffe writes,

> While the histories of left-leaning political women of this period have been recovered, the women who were pro-Treaty, anti-republican, and subsequently involved in the Blueshirts, are still, for the most part missing from our national narrative. Researching the beliefs and ideologies of those women and men, whose convictions led them into proto-fascist organisations, leads to fuller understanding of the political, social, and economic histories of the period.[80]

McAuliffe has been a vocal opponent of the contemporary far right reaction in Ireland and continues to use Irish women's liberation history to confront and undermine the gender critical instrumentalisation of the women's question. In 2023, after the 'women in the home' referendum on Article 41.2 of the Irish constitution seemed to strike a hitch, she wrote,

> The Gov[erment] are cowards, they will not face down the small but vocal far right GCs [Gender Critical Feminists], what they fail to recognise is that the phrase 'women in the home' reflects a gendered marital, domestic and reproduc

tive stereotype. As Hanna Sheehy Skeffington said it was 'anti-woman' & a 'fascist model in which women would be regulated to permanent inferiority.'[81]

The problem in our view is therefore not whether fascist feminism is the correct term for women who find cause with fascism, or whether fascist feminism is a doctrine. We understand fascist feminism as a useful term to consider a historically specific transition from the contingent moral equality of the 19th century women's movements to the reconstruction of the women's cause as fascist. But we also think the term can be understood as a recursive concept and used to consider other novel transitions to fascism, such as gender critical feminism. What defines the gender critical question then is not only the fascist themes reproduced by this cause (or fascists within it) but the fascist instrumentalisation of the women's question and the incredible dangers of that. In this sense, we think fascist feminism is central to antifascism and thinking through and revising the fascist question. In our view, fascist feminism is a recursive phenomenon: fascist feminists are here, and they were always here. And yet women who prospect a fascist feminism or the fascist reconstruction of a feminist issue *cannot exist without the liberal feminist tradition*. The white woman's tradition gave structure to the liberal feminist tradition, to early forms of corporate feminism and imperial feminism in the early 1900s, which can today be advanced by women who are not white. The racialisation of the women's question as white is incredibly significant as it can subsequently function as a progressive relay between various and seemingly incommensurate political traditions and fascism. Tensions that arose within the white women's conjuncture, including colonial, racial and imperial fractures, exemplify the significance of the problem. These tensions determined feminist struggle and produced modes of Black, anti-colonial, decolonial and communist feminism that were the most farsighted and militant of the time. The defeats of social and revolutionary movements, the splits within them, the historical power of racism and fascism to enforce separation cannot be underestimated.

The present is an artefact of these struggles, and our sense of history is lacerated by their defeat. We maintain that there is no straightforward transition from liberalism to fascism or liberal feminism to fascist feminism, but the affinity between early feminism, imperialism and racial nationalism in the progressive era and interwar period *had to be actively and militantly confronted to resist that transition.* This resistance was so often defeated, but how progressive movements split, folded, transitioned or resisted matters greatly as it helps us to define fascism through the political circumstances of a time and place and the particularities of that historical conjuncture. Feminist and indeed trans feminist and queer innovation in theory and history will in turn determine how we all fight today, because concrete viewpoints on class struggle – which refuse the comforts of a single viewpoint, noble canon or undifferentiated lens, but seek to establish the ambivalences of a many sided struggle – course through these conversations and become established within our movements and push on contemporary anti-fascist practices.

Conclusion

Progressive white women struggled to push for reform within white supremacy. Many became insurrectionists and sacrificed their respectability to achieve their aims. White female subjection, the subjection of the 'other half' of the white race, was a major faultline that liberal statesmen such as John Stuart Mill knew had to be reconciled for the liberal tradition to survive. This was clearly not because principles of liberty were hypocritical without women – after all, the majority of women in the empire, and the world, were disregarded. It was because civilisation would be greater with white bourgeois women *on side*. This is less an accusation than a mundane fact. It bears repeating that historical developments of whiteness were reproduced through colonial and settler colonial forms of domination which, as a matter of course, have also been able to recruit women from progressive movements. In colony and in metropole, on plantations,[1] in households, workplaces and high statecraft, white women have for centuries been able to exercise forms of power through inclusion within the ever-shifting identity of whiteness. Women in far right movements have often played, and still play, reproductive, organisational and caring roles that are the lifeblood of movements committed to this civilising project. WKKK and BUF women were prized for their organising and recruiting skills, even while gender segregation and gender roles were emphasised internally even more than they were in the surrounding society. Existing gendered divisions of labour and regulative models of cisnormative complementarity have always been reinforced by far right and fascist politics. White women joined these movements because they were invested in a racist vision, but also because they saw fascism as serving their interests, as being *in defence of them*. They were not dupes, nor were they simply coerced

– even if, as Terese Jonsson has shown of white feminism writ large in her book *Innocent Subjects: Feminism and Whiteness*: 'by investing in discourses of white innocence, white women align themselves with a white supremacist patriarchy in ways which not only enforce the oppression of people of colour, but also their own patriarchal subjugation.'[2]

Fascism and 'progressive relays'

The relationship between white liberal feminism and conservativism has also complicated over time. Historically, much like today, it isn't always easy to clearly demarcate liberal reformist movements and arguments from conservatives and others on the far right (especially those arguments that seek to 'protect' women from racialised threats). The women's cause has developed a system of progressive relays for every possible political tradition, including an archive of justifications for pursuing racist imperialist wars. Liberal progressive defences of women, trans and equal rights can coincide with support for genocidal fascist states, like Israel, without any hint of contradiction, because the racist tradition is so strong in the liberal feminist one. The presence of prominent racialised women in the ranks of the far right also adds to a sense of confusion around race – is white supremacy or white feminism still the right term when so many women of colour take on prominent roles within the far right? In the US, far right figures like African-American Candace Owens, Jewish women like Laura Loomer and Pamela Geller, or a new cohort of Trump-supporting Latina Republicans,[3] all promote white supremacist discourses to advance their careers, to gain power or simply because they believe in it. While the left is constantly faced with splits and the struggle to recompose itself, far right movements seem to strengthen and pluralise through splits that emerge. Owens recently split with parts of the far right because of her stance on Israel, but her support for Palestine has also become the means to promote Catholic antisemitism and anti-communism, broaden her audience and ideological affinities. On the Piers Morgan show, she said,

> When Jewish people die in Israel it is wall to wall coverage,
> but when Christians die all over the world nobody wants to
> talk about it. Everybody wants to correlate everything to
> WWII... [E]veryone wants to talk about Adolf Hitler... [N]-
> obody wants to talk about the Bolsheviks, nobody wants to
> talk about the Christian Holocaust.[4]

That Owens makes a stance against Israel (one that erases the genocide of Palestinians and agency of Palestinian liberation movements) is enough for some on the left to try and reach out. Owens has since interviewed Norman Finkelstein, the son of Holocaust survivors and a leftwing Jewish critic of Israel who is also transphobic.[5] The far right have become experts in affinity (and affiliate) marketing techniques and are constantly looking for opportunities to relay between left, liberal, conservative, and fascist audiences. Unfortunately, many of our most prominent left representatives are yet to realise that the politics only seems to run one way. A year previous to the Finkelstein interview Owens promoted a conspiracy that Dylan Butler, a 17 year old school shooter, who killed one student, one teacher and injured several others before shooting himself, was trans: 'Gender dysphoria is a mental disorder, and the entire LGBTQ movement brought with it a sexual plague on our society.'[6] Finkelstein, incensed and at times lucid on the Zionist instrumentalisation of antisemitism and the manipulation of Holocaust memory, goes the way of so many left intellectuals and academics detached from the struggles of marginalised people they know next to nothing about. Rather than seeking to preserve and therefore differentiate concrete experiences of trans people from the liberal instrumentalisation of identity categories, Finkelstein reacts sporadically to what he sees as another manipulative trend spearheaded by the western media. Above a front cover illustration of a gender nonconforming person in the *New Yorker*, Finkelstein tweets, 'Transgender Cult.'[7]

This monetised media setting seems to scramble many people's expectations of fascism and how a fascist formation manifests because far right compositions are spun chaotically around

rising and falling stars. Many present as 'neither left nor right' including influencers, celebrities, campaigns or 'cancelled' liberals
and leftists seeking new publishing outlets. Far right groups or
movements can often catch alight then fizzle out just as quickly,
only able to cohere around limited goals and loosely networked
communities, before splits occur. These splits suggest new match
ups in a public sphere that borrow from the theatrical duels and
spiritual conversions of the wrestling persona, boxer, or saint.
Ideological relays between liberals, left and the far right, which
are especially well served by this styling of adversarial combat,
are particularly dangerous since, on the left, moral clarity on one
issue can leave audiences with powerful resonances and attach-
ments to an influencer who is clearly a good person and speaks
to a certain truth (and indeed, does this) while co-constituting a
fascist falsehood. We can think here too of how Russell Brand's
conversion from left-wing truth teller and rapist to far right evangelical does not present any contradiction for Finkelstein, who
goes on Brand's show – and will go on any show – since he is
a moral advocate of Palestinian struggle. Finkelstein is uncon-
cerned with how that struggle is being instrumentalised by some
on the far right because his wager is that his skills of moral per-
suasion will bring people on the right side one way or another.[8]

The 'post-ideological' quality of this type of media convergence would seem to end an analogy with the American fascism
of the 1920s, which was particularly conditioned by strict religious sectarianism. Indeed, the incredible breadth of hatreds of
the '100% Americans' of the second KKK developed a movement
that ended up in failure because the rest of America turned on it.
Though it is also true that the religious markets of the 1920s also
had a strong cultural bearing on the adversarial format of the
modern public sphere as such. As Daniel Vaca, who has written
extensively on evangelism and religious markets, writes:

> Difference and debate always had been evangelical obses-
> sions, which publishers and booksellers had acknowledged…
> [The] fundamentalist brand drew its meaning not just from
> the sets of doctrines that fundamentalists claimed … but also

from the contrast that avowed fundamentalists made between themselves and 'modernists.' Throughout the twentieth century, this posture of distinction helped animate evangelical publics, which have taken shape successively around
shared opposition to evolution, alcohol, the New Deal, communism, feminism, desegregation, abortion, same-sex marriage, and more.[9]

How left influencers navigate a public sphere that has a foundation on the religious right and pluralises anti-establishment feel-
ing around international conservative, far right and evangelical
publics – all of which contribute money, fraternities, and leadership candidates to fascist formation – is hardly reflected upon
by those on the left who choose to sail these waters, because to
be part of that dynamic is to be constantly reacting to it. Any
reflection on the gains of such a strategy for liberation, or how
such interventions are attractive to the far right, are hardly un-
derstandable for the individual involved and add up to a politics
that is totally individuated.

There are, then, observable relations between the 21st century fascist formation and the second KKK, but this isn't to say that
nothing new is afoot. American fascism is a confusing picture,
too, because the Democrats have been arming Zionist fascists
while they warn progressives to elect them to save the world
from American fascists. The rise of fascist formations within
liberal democracies is usually interpreted as the warning shot
before a full takeover of the state, but this scenario is neither a
timeless trait of fascism nor always necessary. It is sometimes argued that historical fascism developed in the 1920s to the threat
of communism and no such communist or third worldist movement exists to present that same threat today.[10] That is true in
part, but Israel's genocidal reaction to Hamas and Hezbollah
points to a more classic fascist counterreaction. This time to the
considerable resistance of national liberation struggles in the
Arab region and the threat this poses to US-Israeli occupation.[11]
In the core imperial countries, fascist mobilisation within the police after BLM in 2020 and Stop Cop City is complemented by

respectable forms of liberal state authoritarianism. Meanwhile in Britain, cross party reactions to 'irregular' migration, trans liberation struggles, and ecological activism tend to be legitimised through Mill's 'harm principle' – brutalising people making 'irregular' crossings will 'stop the boats' and therefore prevent further harm; taking healthcare away from trans children is necessary to protect them from the harm they are doing to themselves and harm to others; punishing ecological protestors for shutting down motorways protects the public from harm – because the ambulances can't get through! The western criminalisation of Palestine protests and direct action speaks to a tendency towards ever more aggressive liberal progressive counterinsurgency measures alongside fascist counterreactions. As Jasmine, an Atlanta organiser against Cop City, notes, 'One thing that we talk about a lot in this movement is that the Atlanta Police Department currently trains with the Israeli police, who are practicing genocide against the Palestinian people.'[12]

Fascism, imperialism, fracture

The reason we have chosen to reflect on histories of fracture and division within early feminist movements is not only to investigate parallels and recurrences, but because this historical work is sensitising and humbling and encourages a similar degree of sensitivity to changes of an unexpected nature in the 21st century. The work that social movement historians and historians of social movements put into describing *failures of unity*, in particular, has become completely central to how we address things. *Division* – not parables of unity – free us of doctrinal or teleological thinking about past progressive causes or movements. The findings are often unexpected. Even within white conservative and religious feminist movements, progressive outcomes were struggled for by racialised women who continued to fight against the grain of white supremacy. As we discuss in the first chapter, Black temperance activists rushed to join the ranks of the temperance movement even after Frances Willard's apologism for lynching. This is an insight from historian Ella Wagner that touches on the ambiguities of Jim Crow and the function thereafter of American fascism to enforce it. Black activists in the American South tried to turn temperance concepts of family and nation around to reform projects that provided Black communities with some degree of security from fascism and the nation. The temperance movement splits give us an insight into the struggle to inject antiracism into a reformist white supremacist organisation and the importance of religious movements like this in establishing pockets of community relief from racial segregation. There were also white women who went straight from suffrage or temperance activism, from membership of the Democratic or Republican parties, right into the Ku Klux Klan. Routes into the British Union of Fascists weren't just from suffragism, by any means. Many, many BUF women had been Tories, and a lot came from the Labour Party. While the WKKK met at churches and YWCA buildings, most BUF Women's Section meetings were held in the branch buildings of that most mainstream of organisations: the Women's Institute (WI). Indeed, a useful parallel here can be made between the 'ordinariness' and 'inoffensiveness' of the 'the WI' in the 1930s and the website forum *Mumsnet*[13] and the BBC radio programme *Women's Hour*, which have both been focal points for the growth and radicalisation of gender critical feminism in Britain over the past decade. Cisnormativity is exactly that, *normal*. Being normal is to be against the 'dystopia' of 'gender ideology' and it is this conceit – the normal, everyday reproduction of cisnormativity – that makes contemporary fascist feminism *possible*. A gender critical man or woman and their relation to feminism can therefore be entirely flexible without ever ameliorating the aggressive eliminationist principle that gives gender critical feminism a mission and sense of purpose. Some cadres reject feminism entirely, others disparage it or accuse it of falling from past standards – part of a wider pattern of 'degeneracy.' Uber misogynist men can hurry to the gender critical cause as well as radical feminists of a different time. Some still lay claim to feminism as they do battle for its ownership. All can take as given the *results* and *historical*

representations of past rights struggles and pivot to the liberal my-
thologies projected onto those historic battles on demand. This
can enable gender critical cadres to partake in a variety of political modes and postures that take for granted some measure of
that inheritance.

The ideological currents of early feminism not only prefig-
ure, in specific and limited ways, fascist currents of the 1920s,
but survive as artefacts of the new fascist conjuncture. These
artefacts survive not only because the historical system of racial capitalism survives, just as cisnormativity survives, but also
because historical representations of early feminism give fascist
feminists epidemiological structure and agency to maintain flexible and pragmatic political stances. 'Oikonomic' conceptions of
the household economy that emerged through conservative and
liberal women's movements of the 19th and early 20th century
are being revised by fascist feminists internationally to respond
to a perceived crisis of civilisation as such. These feminist traditions travel, globalise and intersperse within national and regional conjunctures of the far right. Italian prime minister Giorgia
Meloni, for example, justifies the title of anti-feminist. Yet Meloni also reconstructs feminist traditions that have historical form
in liberalism, colonialism, and fascism. She adapts liberal corporate feminist themes in order to find a new equilibrium between
the freedom of women to work and to be homemakers. This reproductivist stance means she can find alliance with the Church,
and a transphobic 'leftwing' Pope, once a sworn enemy.[14] Meloni's ability to bridge the conservative complementarity of the
Church, the corporate feminism of the western liberal tradition
and the fascist feminism of the 'Italian mother' provides her with
the political flexibility to become an ordoliberal broker and make
geopolitical strides.[15] Meloni can agree with Hungarian prime
minister Viktor Orban on family first policies, for example, even
if they disagree on Ukraine. In a speech at the Budapest Demographic Summit, she said,

> The [Hungarian] revolution of 1956 was not only a revolt
> against foreign rule, but also a revolt against those who were

trying to destroy the very foundations of a people's identity: family, religion, national belonging. They are pages of history that cannot be rewritten and no propaganda operation today can ever tear them up. And pages of history that we see again today in Ukraine and that we cannot accept.[16]

We can say, for sure, that Meloni is an enemy of emancipatory feminism, but her Italian 'family-first' policies are also a means to develop fascist feminist positions that triangulate a corporate feminist tradition and a European civilisational femonationalist credo. The appeal to the mother revises a 19th century tradition of the home and nation that prefigured interwar fascist Italy. The appeal to corporate women, as we argue, using the example of Winnifred Harper Cooley, can probably be traced back to the early 1900s and 1910s as questions of industry, production and corporation, were rethought through a modern feminist revision of the *oikos*. This ancient synonym for household management, as Mitropoulos maintains, survives because it is sublimated within the linguistic displacements of modern 'political economy', so that at 'significant junctures ... geopolitical demarcations come to assume the character of a domestic space.'[17]

Meloni has always been a fascist and her recent rise from the fringe shows that fascists can become hegemonic partners within the EU ordoliberal project and progress through the project of 'Fortress Europe' without having to break from it.[18] It is perhaps more complicated to locate and establish the fascist threat when forms of gender critical eliminationism operate deep within the institutional fabric of post-war liberal democracy. We think WKKK histories are instructive, in this sense, because these organisations developed through a particular colonial and liberal democratic setting, where democratic practices were embraced. Unlike interwar Italy, where parliament was dissolved, racial fascism and liberal democratic protocols within the US were intertwined. The 'strength of democracy' – a notion typically understood as a block on authoritarianism – provided the conditions for American fascism within the democratic structure of its pluralities. It is important therefore to consider the advanced development of western liberal democratic infrastructure, including its role in imperial relations, as a condition of contemporary fascism, rather than necessarily a problem for it. The liberal media circuits, commercial media relations and the voluntary and NGO sector provide fascists, evangelical feminists and feminist fascists, with greater flexibility than the programmatic fascist parties or cults of the past. As do church and evangelical fraternal organisations. In the US, the role of natalism and transphobia in the radicalisation of the anti-rights GOP has achieved rapid reversals of rights legislation that no post-civil rights conservative movement has been able to get near to achieving. As Gill-Peterson writes,

> Making policy based in the fantasy that the state can tell the difference between trans and non-trans people is what makes [the 'cis state'] so flexible and resilient. Because it can never successfully do what it promises – draw a hard line between trans and non-trans people – the cis state can ignore all of its failures as equally irrelevant. That is another way of defining impunity.[19]

Moreover, the anti-rights far right of the GOP seem to have no intention of returning to convention (as represented by the 'Never Trumpers'). The 'mama grizzlies' of the Tea Party and the feminine voice of QAnon message-spreading hint at a new fascist women's sphere. Through religious markets, conspiracy markets and influencer platforms emerge a form of commercial fascism that revives the American model of the male fraternity, women's club, cult, grift and racist racket, and becomes a model the international far right can reproduce.

The fraternal organisation of commercial fascism in and within 'advanced democracies' requires us then to assess the empirical fields of fascist formation as they appear and no longer rely on spectrums of 'extremes'. Alongside a class composition analysis of early feminism and fascism in this study, we have therefore been especially interested to concentrate on a historical exchange between liberal progressive and conservative feminist traditions. In particular, secular and religious feminisms in the 19th century and the race and class antagonisms internal to them. These historical precursors cannot alone explain the rise of gender critical feminism, but they can at least remind us to not always think of contradictions within the gender critical cause as inexplicable or necessarily hypocritical or two-faced. The formation of a women's cause can recruit diagonally and across other causes that are logically opposed. It seems hypocritical, for example, that British lesbian radical feminist Julie Bindel and US anti-abortion and anti-LGBTQ+ conservative Jennifer Lahl share a common cause in anti-surrogacy politics and warm relations, sharing selfies and cocktails on social media. Lahl refers to herself as a 'new feminist' who pursues a 'pro-life' conservative activism, but this is modelled around liberal feminist themes of empowerment and anti-exploitation. These conservative initiatives not only anticipated the British gender critical movement but provided ideas, legal infrastructure, funding streams and a public speaking circuit adaptable to (and enthusiastic for) the British anti-trans cause.[20] Gender critical feminism establishes a contingent model of women's unity based on cisnormative, exclusionary premises, and this can hold, despite contradictions internal to it.

Boundary crossing and 'open borders'

It has always been the case that movement failure produces re-actionaries from within the left, but what left ideas were ever the property of the left in the first instance? Feverish critiques of neoliberalism and 'open borders', which have been essential to conservative parts of the left since the 1990s, give structure to anti-establishment writing within the gender critical movement. The need for a strong, moral state to combat the incursions of liberalism has traction in the prose stylings of British self-identifying 'reactionary feminist' Mary Harrington, for instance, who writes,

My first political memory was an epochal one: the fall of the Berlin Wall. The grainy footage of East and West Berliners

in stone-washed denim, hammering at the graffitied concrete that had so long separated them, and pouring through
breaches in Die Mauer to embrace one another, still chokes
me up. That astonishing moment stood, and still stands, as
a governing metaphor for the age that followed: one which
seemed to be all about breaking down walls, and opening everything up. Think of all the nice liberals celebrating 'open'
societies and tutting at 'closed' ones; NGOs such as Open Democracy and Open Society; the respectively positive and negative connotations of 'inclusion', and 'exclusion'. Opening,
expanding, breaking down borders and boundaries is always
better than the inverse. Isn't it?[21]

Melancholy and disappointment at the failure of liberalism to
end history is compounded by a cynical distaste for the fluidity
of 'open' societies. Interviewed for the Anglican weekly, *Church
Times*, Harrington explores her radicalisation to the right:

In the UK, the real hinge moment was what happened immediately after the Crash, when Occupy Wall Street failed.
Because that was the death of the anti-capitalist movement,
such as it was, which I had been a committed part of in my
twenties... It was a strange time. Looking back, in the nough-
ties we thought there was an end to boom-and-bust, and social enterprise was a thing. The Crash killed that for me, as
well as my faith in progress at all. It all imploded at once on
the large as well as the small scale.[22]

Harrington brags that she is now 'smuggling a piece of fairly
straightforward Marxist analysis under the radar into the dark
heart of the American Right',[23] but it would also be too comforting to understand her reactionary feminism as the product
of an appropriation of recent Marxist theories of neoliberalism.
The way Harrington emphasises a deeper logic of open and un-
bounded commodification and its implications for the body and
moral order is far more comparable to the campaigning style of
19th century temperance and purity feminists we looked at in

chapters one and three. It just so happens that many left-wing critiques of neoliberal commodification in the 2000s and 2010s were also unthinkingly reproducing homologies and metaphors of a bad openness and bad boundary crossing to metastasise the ills of globalisation. In truth, reactionary potentials have always been present in vague forecasts of 'commodification' and moralistic critiques of the 'bourgeois individual' prized by some Marxist critics.

A prominent contemporary example of a Marxist left feminist in Britain who has journeyed her way into fascism is Nina Power, for instance. A well-known philosopher and activist on the radical left in the early 2010s, Power campaigned against police violence, wrote feminist books for radical left publishers and hosted radio shows about queer politics. More recently, she has carved out a new career for herself as a gender critical feminist, editing and writing for right-wing newspapers and websites. Again, her appearance and legacy as a progressive feminist have continued to protect her position despite sharing platforms with neo-reactionary advocates of fascist politics. The measure of reputational protection gleaned from being a philosopher, ex-leftist and gender critical feminist, while being found to be propagating outright Nazism, is instructive. Following court revelations that she was running fascist 'groyper' Twitter accounts to bully Jewish artist Luke Turner,[24] and flirting with her fascist boyfriend Daniel 'D.C.' Miller about their enjoyment of *Mein Kampf*, fellow gender critical philosopher Kathleen Stock and others rose to her defence, impervious, or simply accepting of Power's philosophical fascisation. In her dialogues with Miller, Power speculated, 'wonder what the real deal is with the *Protocols [of the Learned Elders of Zion?]*'.[25] The communications between Power and Miller reveal a sniggering, scornful romance over their mutual commitment to pursue every taboo. It is littered with the most abject, one dimensional prejudice. Speculating a new feminism, Power taps, 'no fatties, no women, no homo etc... and definitely definitely no trannies unless it's to admit they are just sick mfs.' Fun, edgy prophecies, 'I think there will be an orgy of blood soon.'[26]

Much of this is directed at former comrades.

People who were close to Power have stated publicly that transphobia and gender critical feminism played a central role in her journey to the far right.[27] It is also instructive that political disillusionment and the bitter partings of ways within progressive causes can provide and have provided, throughout history, powerful 'second winds' of reaction. Rather than think of reaction always through the agency of elites, through concepts of backlash or frontlash from reactionary opponents, or bad faith liberal allies, we should also consider how reactions germinate internally and become reified within the contents of a failed movement, theory set or cause. Harrington and Power, who come from very different progressive traditions (liberal and Marxist respectively) and have their own personal style of argument and presentation, will nonetheless seek to present liberalism and the left as an all-encompassing threat to the individual and moral order as such. As former progressives, they do so with cause, with a new conviction and belief, unlike liberal centrists who cynically drive wedges through the left and move on to reproduce their self-preservation after the fact. Indeed, Power retains a Marxist philosophical critique of individualism which she uses to enliven the spectral theatre of 'gender ideology' and the threat it poses to the nation's children, now for a conservative audience.

A short speech Power gave to the National Conservative (NatCon) conference in 2023 illustrates the opportunities available to progressive philosophers who can cunningly ground fascist desires within a rearticulated moral system. In her talk, 'After the Individual', Power argues that the 'liberal individual' is 'based on a profound misunderstanding,' which 'happened in around 1610.' From this point onwards there is a 'forgetting' of the original meaning of the word individual, which is rather to do with the 'one ... the indivisible.' This distinction is used to relay various atomised expressions of modernity, including young people 'garnering identity' on social media and 'misplaced compassion for meaningless identity categories.' Power stresses her sorrow for such miscalculations, calling them a 'desperate plea for recognition, albeit by identifying themselves into categories, that are unfortunately, incorrect, bureaucratic, consumerist, and algorithmic, and part of the machine that Danny Kruger[28] was talking about earlier.'[29]

Power's argument clearly builds from her training in continental philosophy. The critical emphasis on the individual and reification is suggestive of the influence of Herbert Marcuse and Theodor W. Adorno (whose work has been important to Power in the past) yet is now repackaged for an audience hooked on the threat of 'cultural Marxism'. In this revision the marxist critique of reification relapses into what Adorno himself called the 'language of false escape' – a 'fall back upon the idea of "naturalness", which itself forms a central element of bourgeois ideology'.[30] Power's instrumentalisation of the 'child' is critical to this. She insists,

> I want to say very strongly that children are not individuals… [T]hey need looking after, they do not hold the truth of their identity, we should not be looking at them to tell us who or what they are… [T]hey are vulnerable, and some of the things that are happening to children today are grotesque… [W]e will look back on that with a sense of collective horror because it's our job … *to protect them from themselves, as well as from the culture* [applause].[31]

Power retains her Marxist disdain for liberalism but, through this, the child's vulnerability is romantically coded as the property of responsible owners who, we must assume, populate the NatCon conference; strong and moral parental owners who remain convinced of the need to marshal their children away from harm (ie, from being queer and trans). Indeed, if a child is 'indivisible' – not individual – then they are conveniently released of legal individual rights. Power therefore transfers into philosophical mystification what is more straightforwardly a well-rehearsed far right strategy. In Britain, Gillick's law, the legal principle of consent for under 16-year-olds has been under sustained attack by an alliance of Christian Evangelical and Gender Critical feminists as this allows them to open the door to parental control over the full autonomy and reproductive rights of the child.[32] Power is concerned about bureaucratic identity categories, which are socially produced, but not the moral categories she treats as transcendental. We are told to preserve 'Soul, Character and Responsibility' and release these moral categories from 'identity constraints' as if they are not also identity constraints. The left, her former left, who she believes could not tolerate her own freedom of thought and victimised her for being an eccentric, provide the kernel of danger. Power was cancelled, so ends Marxism:

> The left don't think about class, they don't think about the critique of political economy… [I]t's something else… [W]hat they have accelerated is the smashing of the body, of the destruction of distinction … the relationship between men and women … the reality of sexual difference… [W]e have to know why they've done that.

From indivisibility as 'forgotten' to Marx's 'social individual' Power finds a new feminism of care in

> The Blue Labour project and emphasis on forms of social preservation… [C]onservatism in the true sense … to protect those institutions and forms of belonging that relate to the family, the parish, to all those things that people actually care about… I strongly recommend everyone goes to church, it's fantastic! [applause].[33]

A nuclear family interregnum?

Reactionary oppositions to neoliberalism continue to be reproduced in other styles of aggressively fascist transphobia. The reactionary anti-capitalism of eco-gender critical feminists like Jennifer Bilek, for instance, is funnelled through internet-ready conspiracies about Jewish cabals funding 'transhumanist' plans to turn women into motherless containers for a 'globalist' New World Order. These are not isolated fringe conspiracies. Erstwhile *Economist* journalist, Helen Joyce, now a radicalised anti-trans activist, was accused by Bilek of plagiarism because Joyce's arguments in her *Sunday Times* best seller *Trans* so closely resembled her own.[34] British politicians and prime ministers parrot gender critical feminist positions with increasing regularity and on both sides of the House of Commons trans eliminationism is made into an electoral promise. In the US, Britain and Europe, and other parts of the world, the conspiracy of 'gender ideology' provides one available explanation for the contradictory relationship of capital to the family. As Gleeson and O'Rourke argue, 'the family was supposed to play a dominating role in the stabilisation of capitalism, which in the event exposed its underbelly. Now, many fear, one generation will not follow so easily from the next.'[35] Fascism today is not so much a reaction to a classically revolutionary threat, but one conscious of the limits of democratic appeasement and containment in a world that is invariably more chaotic, or simply breaking down. Yet the late fascist defence of the family is also unable to overcome a nuclear family interregnum peculiar to our time. The untenable combination of pressures and stresses externalised to the nuclear family have contributed to a fascist opportunity. As Jordy Rosenberg writes: 'The family, simply speaking, splinters under the weight of what it has to make up for in the retraction of state resources under austerity.'[36] Pronatalist family friendly policy is posed as a solution to this but can provide nothing qualitatively different to what exists today or has existed before. These ambiguities are compounded by the various levels of abstraction this 'family crisis' presents for liberal governance. The restrictionist tempers of racist politicians are contradicted by a need for immigration in a context of ageing populations. Hence, we see externalisation plans designed to punish the 'boat people' developing alongside more secretive and arcane legal differentiations of visa status to allow temporary visa permits for racialised and gendered service labour. Domestic resolutions of this contradiction are found by impressing ever more violent applications of cisness; to raise, as if by transcendental magic, a cisnormative counter-revolution in gender relations to fix 'demographic decline' in the white world.

With no economic instrument to simultaneously valorise capital and enforce reproductivist order, fascist white replacement fantasies and liberal 'legitimate concerns' writhe around one another in the snake pits of western discourse. As we finish writing this book a wave of racist pogroms targeting Muslims and other people of colour has spread across a Britain, whose history and political-media environment has long threatened another explosion of whiteness riots. The stated fascist justification for the pogroms has been the 'protection of women and girls', and at least some of the gender critical feminists have voiced their support.[37] Where we go from here is uncertain and we must struggle with uncertainty in mind.

Langston Hughes's poem, *Tired*, haunts the era:

I am so tired of waiting,
Aren't you,
For the world to become good
And beautiful and kind?
Let us take a knife
And cut the world in two –
And see what worms are eating
At the rind.[38]

Notes

Introduction

1   Sophie Lewis and Asa Seresin, 'Fascist Feminism: A Dialogue,' *TSQ: Transgender Studies Quarterly*, 9, no. 3 (2022) p. 463.

2   The adoption of the term 'gender critical' provides transphobic public figures with a respectable group identifier. It was partly conceived in reaction to people being called 'TERF' (Trans Exclusionary Radical Feminist). We use 'gender critical' or 'GC' throughout this book because that is how many transphobes, conservatives and fascists want to be identified.

3   Trans Safety Network organisers have, for years now, been contributing anti-fascist research on the convergence of far right and liberal 'gender critical' fronts in Britain. They also cover the British GC relation to anti-trans and anti-rights lobbying internationally. For reports documenting the convergence see: Merle Links and Mallory Moore, 'Gender Critical and Fascist social media increasingly promoting each other,' *Trans Safety Network*, last updated January 22 2022, https://transsafety.network/posts/far-right-converge. See also, Sarah Clarke and Mallory Moore, 'ALERT: Transphobic Feminism and Far Right Activism Rapidly Converging,' *Trans Safety Network*, last updated March 18 2021, https://transsafety.network/posts/gcs-and-the-right.

4   Mallory Moore, 'Gender Ideology? Up Yours!,' *chican3ry*, Patreon, last updated Jan 23 2019, https://chican3ry.medium.com/gender-ideology-up-yours-470575a5311a.

5   Joaquina, 'Analysis: Transphobic social terror and its Nazi origins,' *Trans Safety Network*, September 19 2022, https://transsafety.network/posts/social-terror.

6   'Suella Braverman describes grooming gang comments as "unfashionable facts" after backlash,' *Sky News*, April 20

2023, https://news.sky.com/story/suella-braverman-de-scribes-grooming-gang-comments-as-unfashionable-facts-af-ter-backlash-12861676.

7   Ella Cockbain and Waqas Tufail, 'Failing victims, fuel-ling hate: challenging the harms of the 'Muslim grooming gangs' narrative,' *Race & Class*, 61, no. 3 (2020) accessed on-line 23 September 2024: https://journals.sagepub.com/doi/full/10.1177/0306396819895727.

8   (Content warning) Full article Sarah Champion, 'British Pa-kistani men ARE raping and exploiting white girls… and it's time we faced up to it,' *The Sun*, last updated 18 August 2017, https://www.thesun.co.uk/news/4218648/british-pakistani-men-rap-ing-exploiting-white-girls.

9   (Content warning) For full reference to this fascist propagan-da text, see Peter McLoughlin, *Easy Meat: Inside Britain's Groom-ing Gang Scandal* (Nashville: New English Review Press, 2016) cited in Cockbain and Tufail, 'Failing victims, fuelling hate'.

10   The 'grooming gangs' narrative belongs within a broader tendency to racialise crime in political and popular discourse. The classic example is the racialised panic in 1970s Britain in which young black men were cast as 'muggers.' A reference to Stuart Hall, et al., *Policing the Crisis: Mugging, the State and Law and Order* (London, Macmillan, 1978).

11   'Who is fuelling protests against UK's asylum seekers?,' *Channel 4 News*, last updated 15 March 2023, YouTube, https://www.youtube.com/watch?v=kGbXyWVCqQw&ab_chan-nel=Channel4News.

12   For analysis of Knowsley, the British far right and develop-ments in Ireland see Sophia Siddiqui, 'Attacks on asylum hous-ing: fighting the weaponisation of gender-based violence,' *IRR*, last updated 2 March 2023, https://irr.org.uk/article/from-ire-land-to-knowsley-attacks-on-asylum-housing-and-the-weaponi-sation-of-gender-based-violence. For an analysis of 'whiteness riots,' in respect to British and US colonial settings, see Michael Richmond and Alex Charnley, *Fractured: Race, Class, Gender and*

the Hatred of Identity Politics (London: Pluto Press, 2022), particularly chapters 6 and 7.

13   Turning Point UK was set up by Conservative party donor and son of Conservative Peer, George Farmer. Conservative ministers, Steve Baker, Priti Patel, Jacob Rees Mogg and others praised the organisation when it was announced. See 'Turning Point UK: Conservative Hooligans,' *Red Flare*, last updated 20 June 2024, https://redflare.info/assets/pdfs/Turning_Point_Conservative_hooligans.pdf.

14   Jess O'Thomson, 'The Truth about the Far Right Attack on Honor Oak,' *Trans Safety Network*, last updated 27 June 2023, https://transsafety.network/posts/far-right-attack-on-honour-oak. Turning Point UK's multiracial 'youth' branding had an impressionable impact on some. In 2019, Chris Allen and Ilda Cuko wrote of them, 'While the group has certain leanings and sentiments appropriate to the traditional far right, that they appear so far removed from street-protest groups such as the English Defence League a decade ago, let alone the National Front and Combat 18 "boot boys" of the 1980s, makes it increasingly difficult to comfortably describe them as far right.' At Honor Oak members from all these groups would find each other fighting side by side. Chris Allen and Ilda Cuko, 'Turning Point UK: New Conservative Youth Group Doesn't Fit Understandings of the Far Right,' *The Conversation*, last updated February 14 2019, https://theconversation.com/turning-point-uk-new-conservative-youth-group-doesnt-fit-traditional-understandings-of-the-far-right-111669.

15   Richmond and Charnley, *Fractured*, p. 154.

16   Jules Gill-Peterson, *A Short History of Trans Misogyny* (London: Verso, 2024) p. 33.

17   Ibid, p. 31.

18   Fran Amery refers to GC feminism as a 'biopolitical' project. As she writes, 'beyond direct calls for the surveillance of trans people, gender critical groups also posit trans inclusion as a threat to a broader biopolitical feminist project requiring the

ability to know the differences between men and women in order to govern them.' Fran Amery, '"Gender critical" feminism as biopolitical project,' *Sexualities* (May 2024) accessed online 23 September 2024, https://journals.sagepub.com/doi/full/10.1177/13634607241257397.

19   Gill-Peterson, *A Short History of Trans Misogyny*, p. 142.

20   Ruth Rosen, 'The Tea Party and Angry White Women,' *Dissent Magazine*, accessed 23 September 2024, https://www.dissentmagazine.org/article/the-tea-party-and-angry-white-women.

21   Olivia Rubin and Will Steakin, '"We did our part": The overlooked role women played in the Capitol riot,' *ABC News*, last updated 8 April 2021, https://abcnews.go.com/US/part-overlooked-role-women-played-capitol-riot/story?id=76924779#:~:text=%22Women%20were%20active%20and%20on,or%20dismiss%20these%20as%20exceptions.

22   Jules Gill-Peterson, 'From Gender Critical to QAnon: Anti-Trans Politics and the Laundering of Conspiracy,' *The New Inquiry*, last updated 13 September 2021, https://thenewinquiry.com/from-gender-critical-to-qanon-anti-trans-politics-and-the-laundering-of-conspiracy.

23   Ibid.

24   Serena Bassi and Greta LaFleur, 'Introduction: TERFs, Gender-Critical Movements and Postfascist Feminisms,' *TSQ: Transgender Studies Quarterly* (2022) 9, no. 3, p. 320.

25   See Enzo Traverso, *The New Faces of Fascism: Populism and the Far Right* (London: Verso Books, 2019).

26   Bassi and LaFleur, 'Introduction: TERFs, Gender-Critical Movements,' p. 316-7.

27   Traverso, *The New Faces of Fascism*, p. 13.

28   Ibid, p. 6.

29   Parker's fear of civilisational decline and her concern for protecting 'biologically female-only' spaces led her to call on armed cis men to protect women's bathrooms from the threat of trans

women. See Josh Milton, '"Gender critical feminist" Posie Parker wants men with guns to start using women's toilets,' *Pink News*, January 30 2021, https://www.thepinknews.com/2021/01/30/gender-critical-feminist-posie-parker-men-guns-womens-toilets-twitter.

30   Jess O'Thomson, 'At Kellie Jay Keen's latest rally, only one side was standing for women's rights – and it wasn't Keen's,' *Trans Safety Network*, last updated 9 May 2023, https://transsafety.network/posts/kjk-rally-standing-against-women.

31   (Content warning) 'Kellie-Jay interviewed on Tucker Carlson Today,' *FOX*, 23 May 2022, YouTube, https://www.youtube.com/watch?v=kT262_vpzjI&ab_channel=Kellie-JayKeen.

32   Bassi and LaFleur, 'Introduction: TERFs, Gender-Critical Movements,' p. 325.

33   'Kellie-Jay interviewed on Tucker Carlson'.

34   Fran Amery & Aurelien Mondon, 'Othering, peaking, populism and moral panics: The reactionary strategies of organised transphobia,' *The Sociological Review* (2024). See also Aurelien Mondon and Aaron Winter, *Reactionary Democracy* (London, Verso, 2020).

35   For a recent discussion of the concept of mainstreaming see Katy Brown, Aurelien Mondon and Aaron Winter, 'The far right, the mainstream and mainstreaming: towards a heuristic framework,' *Journal of Political Ideologies*, 9, no. 2, 162–79. See also, Katy Brown, 'Talking "with" and "about" the far right: putting the mainstream in mainstreaming' (PhD diss., Bath University, 2023). Can be accessed online: https://researchportal.bath.ac.uk/en/studentTheses/talking-with-and-about-the-far-right-putting-the-mainstream-in-ma.

36   Cedric Robinson's 'Black construction of fascism' framework helps to seize the term from a European epistemology of fascism and reconsider the racial assembly of the west itself. See Cedric J. Robinson, and Ruth Wilson Gilmore, 'Fascism and the Response of Black Radical Theorists,' in *Cedric J. Robinson: On Racial Capitalism, Black Internationalism, and Cultures of Resis-*

tance, ed. by H. L. T. Quan (London: Pluto Press, 2019) p. 149-59. Thanks to Kian Aspinall whose conversations around Robinson and the tension his work presents for European fascist studies have helped us think about how we approach the study of fascism. Kian is a PhD at Western Sydney University. His thesis is 'Fascism and the Re-Articulation of the Human: Racial Capitalism and the Anti-Fascism of Twentieth Century Black Radical'.

37   David Renton, *The New Authoritarians* (London: Pluto Press, 2019) p. 229.

38   Traverso, *The New Faces of Fascism*, p. 6.

39   Ibid, p. 3.

40   Perry Willson, *Peasant Women and Politics in Fascist Italy* (Abingdon: Routledge, 2003) p. 1.

41   Ibid.

42   Ishay Landa, *The Apprentice's Sorcerer: Liberal Tradition and Fascism* (Leiden: Brill, 2009) p. 3.

43   Not to mention the internet genius who helpfully informs you that 'Nazi did stand for National Socialist, you know.'

44   Within trade union movements there have been many 'anti-socialist socialists' who were fearful of militant socialists and locked out women and the racialised. Landa addresses fascism as a prolonged reaction to the 19th century 'revolt of the masses' and an elitist solution to democratic progress, but there is no substantial analysis of internal divisions and anti-democratic cultures internal to the progressive movements. See Ishay Landa, *Fascism and the Masses: The Revolt against the Last Humans, 1848-1945* (Abingdon: Routledge, 2018).

45   See Cedric Robinson, *An Anthropology of Marxism* (London: Pluto Press, 2019).

46   Even while some in Israel's ruling coalition now wear the identity of 'fascist' with pride. See: Andrew Feinstein, 'Einstein's nightmare: the fascist politicians wielding power in Israel,' *Red Pepper*, last updated 3 November 2023, https://www.redpepper. org.uk/global-politics/palestine-middle-east/einsteins-night-

mare-the-fascist-politicians-wielding-power-in-israel.

47   On Germany, Claudia Koonz, *Mothers in the Fatherland: Women, the Family and Nazi Politics* (New York: St Martins Press, 1987). The majority of our reading has been on the Italian case, Victoria de Grazia, *How Fascism Ruled Women: Italy, 1922-1945* (Berkeley: University of California Press, 1992). See also Perry Willson's *Peasant Women and The Clockwork Factory: Women and Work in Fascist Italy* (Oxford: Clarenden Press, 1993). For an analysis of gender, Gaia Giuliani, *Race Nation and Gender in Modern Italy: Intersectional Representations in Visual Culture* (London, Palgrave, 2019). European overview, Kevin Passmore, ed. *Women, Gender, and Fascism in Europe, 1919-1945* (New Brunswick, NJ: Rutgers University Press, 2003).

48   Kathleen Blee, 'Where Do We Go from Here? Positioning Gender in Studies of the Far Right,' *Politics, Religion & Ideology*, 21, no. 4 (2020) p. 419.

49   Ibid, p. 430.

50   A review of contemporary debates around this problem, including our own approach: Andrei Belibou, 'Co-opting and being co-opted: on critiques of identity politics,' *Distinktion: Journal of Social Theory* (2024) p. 1-23.

51   We have written a relatively short compositionist analysis that could not do justice to the personal and affective aspects of the early feminist movements. However, we think Hemmings establishes a standard of left wing reflexivity and critical seriousness here that is important to consider. Clare Hemmings, 'A Feminist Politics of Ambivalence: Reading with Emma Goldman,' *Revista Estudos Feministas*, 26, no. 3 (2018).

52   Thanks to Mallory Moore, in particular, for her feedback on the original text. Also, Jaemie, for their perspectives on trans struggle, the anti-fascist stand at Hyde Park and Honor Oak, and all our other conversations. And many long conversations with Kell on a Friday at 56a.

1. US Suffragism and Temperance

1   Robert O. Paxton, 'The Five Stages of Fascism,' *The Journal of Modern History*, 70, no. 1 (1998) p. 12.

2   George Jackson, *Blood in My Eye* (New York: Random House, 1973).

3   Ibid, p. 72.

4   Thomson Reuters, 'New York governor apologizes for implying it is "Israel's right" to destroy Gaza,' *CBC*, last updated 17 February 2024, https://www.cbc.ca/news/world/new-york-governor-apologizes-israel-gaza-canada-buffalo-kathy-hochul-1.7118711.

5   Paxton, 'The Five Stages of Fascism,' p. 14.

6   Elizabeth Cady Stanton, 'Declaration of Sentiments,' accessed online, https://www.loc.gov/exhibitions/women-fight-for-the-vote/about-this-exhibition/seneca-falls-and-building-a-movement-1776-1890/seneca-falls-and-the-start-of-annual-conventions/declaration-of-sentiments.

7   See 'Frederick Douglass speaks in support,' *The North Star*, 28 July 1848, accessed online: https://www.loc.gov/exhibitions/women-fight-for-the-vote/about-this-exhibition/seneca-falls-and-building-a-movement-1776-1890/seneca-falls-and-the-start-of-annual-conventions/frederick-douglass-speaks-in-support.

8   See Angela Davis, *Women, Race and Class* (New York: Vintage Books, 1983) p. 59.

9   See David Roediger, *Seizing Freedom: Slave Emancipation and Liberty For All* (London: Verso, 2015).

10   Quoted in, Lauri Umansky, co-editor with Paul K. Longmore, Michele Plott, *Making Sense of Women's Lives: An Introduction to Women's Studies* (London: Rowman & Littlefield Publishers, 2000) p. 392.

11   Elizabeth Cady Stanton, Susan B. Anthony, Matilda J. Gage,

History of Woman Suffrage Volume One (Rochester: Susan B. Anthony, 1881). Open source e-book access https://tinyurl.com/yckknzcp.

12   Quoted in Nell Irvin Painter, *Sojourner Truth: A Life, A Symbol* (New York: W. W. Norton & Company, 1997) p. 225.

13   Richard Galant, 'For women, a seat at the table,' *CNN*, last updated 8 December 2010, https://edition.cnn.com/2010/OPINION/12/08/pelosi.ted.women/index.html.

14   Painter, *Sojourner Truth*, p. 231.

15   Quoted in, Davis, *Women, Race and Class*, p. 76.

16   Ibid, p. 76.

17   Charles W Mills, 'Racial Liberalism,' *PMLA*, 123, no. 5 (2008) p. 1383.

18   Ellen Carol DuBois, *Woman Suffrage and Women's Rights* (New York: NYU Press, 1998) p. 69.

19   Davis, *Women, Race and Class*, p. 122.

20   Carrie Chapman Catt, 'Presidential Address to NAWSA – May 30, 1901,' *Archive of Women's Political Communication*. Can be accessed online: https://awpc.cattcenter.iastate.edu.

21   Davis, *Women, Race and Class*, p. 123.

22   Davis, *Women, Race and Class*, p. 125.

23   Allison L. Sneider, *Suffragists in an Imperial Age: U.S. Expansion and the Woman Question, 1870-1929* (Oxford: Oxford University Press, 2008) p. 5-6.

24   DuBois, *Woman's Suffrage and Women's Rights*, p. 70.

25   Elizabeth Cady Stanton, Susan B. Anthony, Matilda J. Gage, *History of Woman Suffrage Volume Two* (Rochester: Susan B. Anthony, 1882) p. 864. Open source e-book https://tinyurl.com/4263dv8u.

26   As Noel Ignatiev points out in his study of how the Irish became white: if this was a point of principle then the same Republican power brokers would have brought the same energy to ensuring the voting rights of Black minority communities in

northern states. But they didn't. 'After the Civil War, Southern recalcitrance pushed the Republican Party to embrace Negro suffrage in the South (although many Republicans continued to oppose it in the North).' Noel Ignatiev, *How The Irish Became White* (New York: Routledge, 1995) p. 190.

27   Winnifred Harper Cooley, Carrie Chapman Catt, and National American Woman Suffrage Association Collection, *The New Womanhood* (New York: Broadway Publishing Company, 1904) p. 6. Can be accessed online: https://www.loc.gov/item/04037023.

28   Jane Mansbridge and Katherine Flaster, 'Male Chauvinist, Feminist, Sexist, And Sexual Harassment: Different Trajectories In Feminist Linguistic Innovation,' *American Speech*, 80, no. 3 (2005) p. 265.

29   Ibid.

30   Cooley et al., *The New Womanhood*, p. 95-6.

31   Ibid, p. 21.

32   Ibid, p. 92.

33   Ibid, p. 102.

34   Interview with Angela Mitropoulos, 'On Borders / Race / Fascism / Labour / Precarity / Feminism / etc.,' *Base Publication*, last updated 29 October 2016, https://www.basepublication.org/?p=107.

35   Cooley et al., *The New Womanhood*, p. 136.

36   Ishay Landa, *Fascism and the Masses* (New York: Routledge, 2018) p. 16.

37   David Renton, *The New Authoritarians*, p. 12.

38   Cooley et al., *The New Womanhood*, p. 92.

39   Angela Mitropoulos, 'Fascism, from Fordism to Trumpism,' *s0metim3s*, last updated 17 December 2015, https://s0metim3s.com/2015/12/17/fascism-from-fordism-to-trumpism. See also Angela Mitropoulos, *Contract and Contagion: From Biopolitics to Oikonomia* (London: Pluto Press, 2012).

40   Cooley et al., *The New Womanhood*, p. 34.

41   Melissa Cooper, *Family Values: Between Neoliberalism and the New Conservatism* (New York: Zone Books, 2017) p. 78.

42   See, for example, Jack S. Blocker, 'Separate Paths: Suffragists and the Women's Temperance Crusade,' *Signs*, 10, no. 3 (1985) p. 460-76. Blocker emphasises some important differences. For an alternative perspective see Ruth Bordin, *Frances Willard: A biography* (Chapel Hill: University of North Carolina, 1986). Bordin shows, for example, how Women's Christian Temperance Union (WCTU) leader Frances Willard was not personally wary of suffrage but feared religiously conservative North Mid Westerners – who had flocked to the WCTU during the 1873-74 surge – might be alienated from the alignment.

43   Richard H. Chused, 'The Temperance Movement's Impact on Adoption of Women's Suffrage,' *Akron Law Review*, 53, no. 2, p. 361.

44   This membership estimation is inclusive of auxiliaries, such as the Young Women's Christian Temperance Union. Ruth Bordin, *Woman and Temperance: The Quest for Power and Liberty, 1873 to 1900* (Philadelphia: Temple University Press, 1981) p. 3-4.

45   Suzanne M. Marilley, 'Frances Willard and the Feminism of Fear,' *Feminist Studies*, 19, no. 1 (1993) p. 131.

46   Frances Willard, 'Temperance and Home Protection,' *Archives of Women's Political Communication*. Transcript of speech delivered at Newark, January 1st, 1876. Can be accessed online: https://awpc.cattcenter.iastate.edu/2020/11/04/temperance-and-home-protection-1876.

47   Ibid.

48   Marilley, 'Frances Willard,' p. 126.

49   Marilley, 'Frances Willard,' p. 123.

50   Marilley refers to Temperance suffragism as a 'feminism of fear' distinct from a 'feminism of rights' (women's suffrage). Marilley, 'Frances Willard', p. 125. The WCTU also had a significant impact on the rise of the Prohibition Party. The latter

supported suffrage to attract WCTU members to its ranks. See Adam Chamberlain, Alixandra B. Yanus, Nicholas Pyeatt, 'The Connection Between the Woman's Christian Temperance Union and the Prohibition Party,' *SAGE Open*, 6, no. 4 (2016).

51   As Susan Levine explains, 'In many working-class communities the saloon was the traditional meeting place for trade unions as well as for political organisations. Lady Knights, and a significant number of men, argued that using the saloon as a meeting place not only gave support to the monopolistic brewing interests but also encouraged division within the family by separating the husband from his wife and children. The Knights proposed their own local assemblies as alternatives to saloon culture and posed their movement as the alternative focus for working-class community life. Willard noted the success of this effort, saying, "The Local Assembly in every town and village draws young men away from the saloon, its debates help to make them better citizens, and that the mighty Labor movement has, by outlawing the saloon socially, done more for temperance than we who devote our lives to its propaganda have been able to achieve in the same period."' Susan Levine, 'Labor's True Woman: Domesticity and Equal Rights in the Knights of Labor,' *The Journal of American History*, 70, no. 2 (1983) p. 338.

52   Levine, 'Labor's True Woman,' p. 337.

53   Chused calls this, 'one of the most interesting responses ... reported in a letter from Miriam M. Cole that was transcribed by Elizabeth Cady Stanton, Susan B. Anthony, and Matilda Joslyn Gage and published in the History of Woman Suffrage well after the Crusades ended.' Chused, 'The Temperance Movement's Impact,' p. 370.

54   Stanton didn't like that it was unlawful. 'This "whisky war," as now waged,' she said, 'is mob law, nothing more nor less, and neither church influence, psalms nor prayers can sanctify it. Though we may wink at mob law in a good cause, we are educating the people to use it in a bad one.' Cited in Blocker, 'Separate Paths,' p. 468.

55   Quoted in Kenneth Rose, *American Women and the Repeal of Prohibition* (New York: New York University Press, 1996) p. 26.

56   Willard quoted in Vron Ware, *Beyond The Pale* (London: Verso Books, 2015) p. 200.

57   Ibid, p. 169-224.

58   Ella Wagner, '"The Saloon Is Their Palace": Race, Immigration, and Politics in the Woman's Christian Temperance Union, 1874-1933,' (Ph.D. diss., Loyola University Chicago, 2022) p. 153. Can be accessed online: https://ecommons.luc.edu/luc_diss/3956.

59   Wagner, 'The Saloon Is Their Palace,' p. 113.

60   Ibid.

61   Ibid, p. 158.

62   Ibid, p. 157.

63   Ibid, p. 164.

64   Davis, *Women, Race and Class*, p. 195

65   Bell Hooks, *Ain't I A Woman* (London: Pluto Press, 1987) p. 170.

66   Wagner, 'The Saloon Is Their Palace,' p. 188.

2. The Women of the Ku Klux Klan

1   (Content warning) Daisy Douglas Barr, 'The Soul of America,' in *Papers read at the meeting of Grand Dragons, Knights of the Ku Klux Klan, at their first annual meeting held at Asheville, North Carolina, July, 1923: together with other articles of interest to Klansmen* (1923). Can be accessed online: https://digital.lib.ecu.edu/11176, p. 135.

2   After two years of appeals, Governor John M. Slaton commuted Frank's sentence from death to life imprisonment. Frank had already survived his throat being slit by another prisoner before he was eventually kidnapped from prison and lynched. For a primer see, 'The Lynching of Leo Frank,' *History.com*, last

updated 6 April 2023, https://www.history.com/topics/early-20th-century-us/leo-frank-lynching.

3   For a comprehensive study of the KKK as a commercial business venture see Charles C. Alexander, 'Kleagles and Cash: The Ku Klux Klan as a Business Organization, 1915-1930,' *The Business History Review*, 39, no. 3 (1965) p. 348-67.

4   Nancy MacLean, *Behind The Mask of Chivalry* (Oxford: Oxford University Press, 1994) p. 116.

5   Frances E Willard, *Home protection manual: containing an argument for the temperance ballot for woman, and how to obtain it, as a means of home protection; also constitution and plan of work for state and local W. C. T. unions* (New York: 'The Independent' office, 1879). Can be accessed online: https://www.loc.gov/item/09034897/.

6   Womans Christian Temperance Union, Indiana, and Stella C Stimson, Twenty lessons on government; ten lessons in Indiana government (Indiana: Womans Christian temperance union of Indiana, 1919). Can be accessed online: https://www.loc.gov/item/20003897.

7   Ibid.

8   Ibid.

9   Kathleen M. Blee, *Women of the Klan: Racism and Gender in the 1920s* (California: University of California Press, 2009) p. 2.

10   Blee, *Women of the Klan*, p. 29. See also Ryan Driskell Tate, 'Lulu Alice Boyers Markwell (1865–1941),' *Encyclopaedia of Arkansas*, last updated 29 August 2024, https://encyclopediaofarkansas.net/entries/lulu-alice-boyers-markwell-7440.

11   Quoted in Blee, *Women of the Klan*, p. 32.

12   Ibid.

13   Ibid, p. 105.

14   Ibid, p. 110.

15   Kathleen M. Blee and Kimberly A. Creasap, 'Conservative and Right-Wing Movements,' *Annual Review of Sociology*, 36 (Au-

gust 2010) p. 274.

16   Large protests disrupted the annual gala of the Moms For Liberty in Philadelphia in the summer of 2023. Ron De Santis and Donald Trump were keynote speakers. See Kate Edwards, '"Fascists Go Home!": Philadelphians Reject Far Right "Moms for Liberty",' *truthout.org*, last updated 3 July 2023, https://truthout.org/articles/fascists-go-home-philadelphians-reject-far-right-moms-4-liberty.

17   Michael Newton, *White Robes and Burning Crosses: A History of the Ku Klux Klan from 1866* (North Carolina: McFarland & Company, 2014) p. 51.

18   Laura Smith, 'The Truth About Women and White Supremacy,' *The Cut*, last updated 13 August 2017, https://www.thecut.com/2017/08/charlottesville-attack-women-white-supremacy.html.

19   Blee, *Women of the Klan*, p. 28.

20   Blee, *Women of the Klan*, p. 1.

21   Cooley et al., *The New Womanhood*, p. 60.

22   Ibid, p. 122.

23   Ibid, p. 70.

24   Dwight W. Hoover, 'Daisy Douglas Barr: From Quaker to Klan "Kluckeress",' *Indiana Magazine of History*, 87, no. 2 (1991) p. 173.

25   Ibid, p. 189.

26   See Justin Clark, 'The Indianapolis Times: A Short History,' *Hoosier State Chronicles*, last updated 13 April 2017, https://blog.newspapers.library.in.gov/tag/ku-klux-klan.

27   Linda Gordon, 'The Second Coming of the KKK,' 29 October 2018, *Ottoman History Podcast*, Length in 25:35. Can be accessed online: https://soundcloud.com/ottoman-history-podcast/the-second-coming-of-the-kkk-linda-gordon. See also Linda Gordon, *The Second Coming of the KKK: The Ku Klux Klan of the 1920s and the American Political Tradition* (New York: Liveright,

2017).

28   See Stephen J. Taylor, 'A Ku Klux Quaker?,' *Historic Indianapolis*, last updated 28 September 2015, https://historicindianapolis.com/a-ku-klux-quaker. See also Theo Anderson, 'Back Home Again (and Again) in Indiana: E. Howard Cadle, Christian Populism, and the Resilience of American Fundamentalism,' *Indiana Magazine of History*, 102, no. 4 (2006) p. 301-38. The Cadle Tabernacle Audio Collection is archived by the Fuller David Allan Hubbard Library and can be accessed online: https://cdm16677.contentdm.oclc.org/digital/collection/p16677coll8.

29   Anderson, 'Back Home Again,' p. 317-8.

30   'Citizenship in the Invisible Empire was expensive. The initiation fee, purchase of a robe, and payment of taxes really marked but the beginning of the Klan's financial demands on the ordinary Knight.' Alexander, 'Kleagles and Cash,' p. 360.

31   Indeed, the 1920s KKK were ensconced in commercial grifts and scandals much like the contemporary 'Post-Internet Far Right' are today and this presented similar organising dilemmas. See Alex Roberts and Sam Moore, *Post-Internet Far Right: Fascism in the Age of the Internet* (London: Dog Section Books, 2021).

32   David A. Horowitz, 'Social Morality and Personal Revitalization: Oregon's Ku Klux Klan in the 1920s,' *Oregon Historical Quarterly*, 90, no. 4 (1989) p. 365-84.

33   We look at histories of American nativism and the anti-Chinese campaigns of the Knights in particular in other work. See Richmond and Charnley, *Fractured*, p. 123-49.

34   (Content warning) Hiram Wesley Evans, 'The Klan's Fight for Americanism,' *The North American Review*, 223, no. 830 (1926) p. 52.

35   Ibid.

36   Thomas R. Pegram, 'The Ku Klux Klan, Labor, and the white working class during the 1920s,' *The Journal of the Gilded Age and Progressive Era*, 17, no. 2 (2018) p. 374.

37   Quoted in Kathleen M. Blee, 'Women in the 1920s' Ku Klux Klan Movement,' *Feminist Studies*, 17, no. 1 (Spring, 1991) p. 58.

38   This 'sellers of sex' moral panic was racialised around Jewish sellers of pornography in the Lower East Side of New York. Because Jewish minorities (typically poor Jews recently arrived from Europe) were, along with other European immigrants, selling erotica, anti-Semitic 'white slave trade' stereotypes became established fare. Jay Gertzman includes the erotica dealer within his suggestive concept of the 'pariah capitalist' – a predatory capitalist associated with the new immigrant entrepreneurs, racial stereotypes of the Jewish 'parvenu', and 'social climbers', who were bringing the morals of the country into disrepute. Gertzman gives an account of the complexities of the phenomenon in his *Bookleggers and Smuthounds: Trade in Erotica, 1920-40* (Philadelphia: University of Pennsylvania Press, 2001).

39   Simmons, Tyler and Clarke had all previously been in fraternal organisations – popular among early 20th century white Americans. Miguel Hernandez argues that the second KKK targeted the masonic movement, amongst other fraternal organisations, to recruit new members and this sometimes produced great friction within the lodges. Miguel Hernandez, 'Fighting Fraternities: The Klu Klux Klan and Freemasonery in 1920s America' (Ph.D. diss., Exeter University, 2014).

40   MacLean, *Behind The Mask*, p. 10.

41   Nancy MacLean on the breadth and scale of the Klan's reach in this period: 'state and local Klans published some forty weekly newspapers' and with a national lecture bureau 'its speakers addressed audiences of well over 200,000 people.' MacLean, *Behind The Mask*, p. 10.

42   Hernandez, 'Fighting Fraternities,' p. 70.

43   Matt Blum, '1927 news report: Donald Trump's dad arrested in KKK brawl with cops,' *Boing boing*, last updated 9 September 2015, https://boingboing.net/2015/09/09/1927-news-report-donald-trump.html.

44   'In 1925, when the movement was in decline, more than

twenty percent of Indiana's native-born white men were still members of the Klan. This and other evidence leads to a conservative estimate that between one quarter and one third of Indiana's native white men had been members of the movement at its zenith.' Leonard J. Moore, 'Review of Historical Interpretations of the 1920's Klan: The Traditional View and the Populist Revision, by David H. Bennett and Wyn Craig Wade,' *Journal of Social History*, 24, no. 2 (1990) p. 352. See also Leonard J. Moore, 'White Protestant Nationalism in the 1920's: The Ku Klux Klan in Indiana' (Ph.D. diss., University of California, Los Angeles, 1985).

45   MacLean, *Behind The Mask*, p. 81.

46   In both Republican and Democratic National conventions in 1924, the Klan impressed considerable influence on candidate nominations. See Rory McVeigh, 'Power Devaluation, the Ku Klux Klan, and the Democratic National Convention of 1924,' *Sociological Forum*, 16, no. 1 (2001) p 1-30.

47   MacLean writes, 'The typical Klansman was not simply petit-bourgeois; he appeared less economically secure than the norm for his class... They were especially anxious to distinguish themselves – particularly through their moral codes – from the ordinary workers they viewed as beneath them.' *Behind The Mask*, p. 58. For a discussion of MacLean's contribution to Klan historiography and challenges to it see Thomas Pegram's 'Afterword: Historians and the Klan,' in *One Hundred Percent American: The Rebirth and Decline of the Klu Klux Klan in the 1920* (Chicago: Ivan R. Dee, 2011) p. 221-9.

48   Kenneth C Barnes writes, 'In addition to officeholders, the Klan membership included the professional and business leaders of the community, as well as the most prosperous farmers in the surrounding areas. The forty-six farmers constituted the largest occupational category... Most of these farmers were anything but subsistence agriculturalists. Eight described themselves as orchardists, involved in the countries' commercial fruit business. One of these, William Erwin Ammons, had lived in the

Peel House, a fourteen-room mansion just west of Bentonville and today a historic site and museum.' Kenneth C Barnes, 'Another Look behind the Masks: The Ku Klux Klan in Bentonville, Arkansas, 1922-1926,' *The Arkansas Historical Quarterly*, 76, no. 3 (2017) p. 197.

49   Pegram, 'The Ku Klux Klan,' p. 377.

50   Ibid, p. 384-5.

51   Moore offers an extensive review of the literature and argues that studies of social composition in the surviving membership lists show that Klansmen 'generally made up an occupational and religious cross-section of white Protestant society.' Moore, 'Review of Historical Interpretations', p. 352. Further, 'The Klan appears to have acted as a kind of interest group for the average white Protestant who believed that his values should be dominant in American society.' p. 354. Moore therefore refers to the KKK as 'populist' and opposes this to 'nativist' interpretations that had understood the KKK as fringe. This can lead us into some confusion, however. It is difficult to find an American populist movement in the 19th century that did not organise itself around nativist themes. MacLean's conception of the Klan as a form of 'reactionary populism' offers more clarity in our view because it clarifies the limited role of a 'people' within it. See Nancy MacLean, Aimee Imlay and Matthew Wentz, 'Reactionary Populism and the Historical Erosion of Democracy in America: An Interview with Nancy MacLean,' *disClosure: A Journal of Social Theory*, 29, no. 13 (2020). 'American fascism' is in our view appropriate for the second KKK.

52   MacLean, *Behind The Mask*, p. 54.

53   The KKK tended to explain class conflict through racialisation. The problem of the labouring class was a problem of inferior, immoral, rabble-rousing or feckless workers (immigrant or Black depending on local context). In Western states, Mormons and Chinese-Americans were also targeted. The enemy above was brought about by an all-dominating Jewish control.

54   It was not the same racial worldview in the Italian case

though. The Italian *stirpe* (meaning lineage, descendance) was reflective of a regional proximity to Africa and therein a racial distinction developed between Northern and Southern Italians. Italian fascists went some way to expanding the racial console of the *stirpe* through spiritual renditions of nationalism (even as these regional asymmetries were maintained). See Edoardo Marcelli Barsotti, 'Race and Risorgimento: An Unexplored Chapter of Italian History,' *Journal of Modern Italian Studies*, 25 no. 3 (2020). See also, Barbara Sorgoni, 'Italian Anthropology and the Africans: The Early Colonial Period,' in Patrizia Palumbo (ed), *A Place in the Sun: Africa in Italian Colonial Culture From Post-Unification to the Present* (Berkeley: University of California Press, 2003).

55   The KKK's anti-Catholicism was based on a crude dual loyalty basis – that Catholic Americans were pawns of the pope. American fascism was also emerging within Catholic communities. Father Coughlin, for example, who was a prominent Catholic radio propagandist, praised Mussolini and Hitler but railed against the KKK. Antisemitic conspiracy theory was key to his success. He turned away from FDR New Dealism based on a Jewish banking obsession, spread 'Judeo-Bolshevism' conspiracies that Jewish bankers were behind the Russian revolution and spread the *Protocols of the Learned Elders of Zion*. There is also some evidence Coughlin received funding from Nazi Germany. Cedric Robinson looks at the contribution of Italian American elites to fascism in America. See, Cedric. J. Robinson, 'The African diaspora and the Italo-Ethiopian crisis,' *Race & Class*, 27, no. 2 (1985) p. 51-65. On Coughlin in particular see: Charles J. Tull, *Father Coughlin and the New Deal* (New York: Syracuse University Press, 1965).

56   For a comprehensive history on the market segmentation of the American evangelical tradition see Daniel Vaca, *Evangelicals Incorporated* (Cambridge: Harvard University Press, 2019).

57   See Philip Morgan, *Fascism in Europe, 1919-1945* (Abingdon: Routledge, 2003).

58   As described by a fascist participant on the March to Rome,

Curzio Malaparte in *The Technique Of Revolution* (Aurora: Morris Productions, 2004). Can be accessed online: https://archive.org/details/malaparte-curzio-coup-detat-the-technique-of-revolution-2004/page/n5/mode/2up.

59   Paxton, *Anatomy of fascism*, p. 72-3.

60   'But, more fundamentally, his policies represented his political instincts and presentational requirements, less so a long-term economic strategy.' Peter J. Williamson, *Duce: The Contradictions of Power* (London: Hurst Publishers, 2023) p. 164.

61   In the early days, Mussolini attempted to take over local cultural centres to establish control throughout the regions, 'Many of the organisations that provided Opera Nazionale Dopolavoro (OND) services were existing local associations such as choral societies or theatre groups – of which there were many – that the Fascists simply took over. These organisations were not particularly Fascist in character, leading to membership tests to allow in only those who demonstrated the necessary allegiance to the regime.' Ibid, p. 202.

62   In the 1930s, Partito Nazionale Fascista (PNF) bodies attempted to mediate and control provincial prefects, however, 'The predominant position in the provinces was an ongoing tension-cum-conflict between the prefects and the federale (local PNF leader), particularly over appointments. The central state could partially manage, but never eradicate, these stresses. PNF penetration of the local state at best proved limited.' Ibid, p. 101.

63   Fascist settler colonisation in Libya in the 1930s was an attempt to rekindle enthusiasm for the imperial promise of the fascist project. This included resettlement schemes for Italians that lasted into the 1960s. See Pamela Ballinger, 'Colonial Twilight: Italian Settlers and the Long Decolonization of Libya,' *Journal of Contemporary History*, 51, no. 4 (2016) p. 813-38.

64   As explored in Thomas Brook, 'The Clansman's Race-Based Anti-Imperialist Imperialism,' *The Mississippi Quarterly*, 62, no. 2 (2009) p. 303-33.

65   See the following for historical studies of two figures from

Fasci Femminili and surrounding literature on the organisation. Perry Willson, 'A "Shining Example of Fascist Womanhood": Angiola Moretti 1925-1943,' *European History Quarterly*, 52, no. 4 (2022) p. 744-67. See also Perry Willson, 'The Fairytale Witch: Laura Marani Argnani and the Fasci Femminili of Reggio Emilia, 1929-1940,' *Contemporary European History*, 15, no. 1 (2006) p. 23-42.

66   'City and rural county newspapers of the time were full of notices for meetings of women to discuss immigration restrictions, the virtues of Protestantism, Prohibition, national pride, declining public morality, the 'godlessness' of public school teaching, the impending threat posed by immigrating radicals, and how to exercise newly granted voting rights in a patriotic, God-fearing direction.' Blee, *Women of the Klan*, p. 122.

67   Ibid.

68   Blee, 'Women in the 1920s,' p. 67.

69   Ko Bragg, 'First came suffrage. Then came the Women of the Ku Klux Klan,' *The 19th*, last updated 28 December 2020, https://19thnews.org/2020/12/first-came-suffrage-then-came-the-women-of-the-ku-klux-klan.

70   Blee, *Women of the Klan*, p. 154-55.

71   Walter White, *Rope and Faggot: A Biography of Judge Lynch* (New York: AA Knopf, 1929) p. 120.

72   Strongholds of the KKK were often in places that were homogenously white Protestant. Yet even where there was a small minority Catholic, Jewish or Black community, these local 'threats' were identified as symptoms of growing infiltration. A sample of regional studies: Richard Mark Paul, '"This Is Not a Catholic Nation": The Ku Klux Klan Confronts Franco-Americans in Maine', *The New England Quarterly*, 82, no. 2 (2009) p. 285-303. Chris Rhomberg, 'White Nativism and Urban Politics: The 1920s Ku Klux Klan in Oakland, California,' *Journal of American Ethnic History*, 17, no. 2 (1998) p. 39-55. Eckard V Toy, 'The Ku Klux Klan in Tillamook, Oregon,' *The Pacific Northwest Quarterly*, 53, no. 2 (1962) p. 60-4.

73   Blee, *Women of the Klan*, p. 155.

74   Erin Blakemore, '"Ku Klux Kiddies": The KKK's Lit-tle-Known Youth Movement', *History.com*, last updated, 26 June 2019, https://www.history.com/news/kkk-youth-recruitment-1920s.

75   Blee, *Women of the Klan*, p. 171.

76   MacLean, *Behind The Mask*, p. 17. See also Blee, *Women of the Klan*, p. 3, 115, 148-9.

77   'In 1923, for example, at least seventy-five congressional representatives were said to owe their seats to the Klan... The Klan held sway in the political life of many states; it dominated some outright, such as Indiana and Colorado.' MacLean, *Behind The Mask*, p. 17-8.

78   'The Klan were able to operate in many areas with near impunity. With powerful Klan members and allies in law enforcement, Protestant churches and the judiciary as well as cowed, quiescent or supportive whites in newspapers, education and beyond, fighting back against them, for the few who tried, was a dangerous, often a losing, battle.' MacLean, *Behind The Mask*, p. 18.

79   Electoral respectability was a concrete aim of the second KKK and they often organised around various social issues. The vigilantism of the second Klan should also not be obscured by this. As MacLean writes, 'Klan leaders did repeatedly deny that their movement engaged in extralegal activity, and the historian cannot simply ignore these disavowals. But to accept them at face value would be naive and dangerous... The occasions of such denials were also important. They usually came after the public revelation of some vigilante activity attributed to the Klan.' MacLean, *Behind the Mask*, p. 166. Another period of Klan vigilantism that is overshadowed by treating the second KKK as a self-evidently 'mainstream' outfit is that of the 'Black Legion', which grew out of disillusionment with the commercial recruitment model of 1921-1925. See Peter H Amann, 'Vigilante Fascism: The Black Legion as an American Hybrid,' *Comparative*

Studies in Society and History, 25, no. 3 (1983) p. 490-524.

80   Speaking to *USA Today* in 2018 is Avilae Horton, a co-organiser of the Unite The Right demonstration a year on from fascists marching through Charlottesville and Heather Heyer being murdered. 'Multiple women have been instrumental in planning this year's rally,' Horton said. The 21-year-old said the 12-person team is almost split between men and women.' Marina Pitofsky, 'Are women changing "Unite the Right" or just "rebranding" the movement?', *USA Today News*, accessed online 27 September 2024, https://eu.usatoday.com/story/news/2018/08/09/women-unite-right-rally-2018/874631002.

81   Rachel Leah, '"Alt-right" women are upset that "alt-right" men are treating them terribly,' *Salon*, last updated 4 December 2017, https://www.salon.com/2017/12/04/alt-right-women-are-upset-that-alt-right-men-are-treating-them-terribly.

82   Anne Marie Waters, a far right leader in Britain, has made similar comments, saying of far right men: 'You've got to contain yourself, 'cause if you get angry, they'll be like, oh hysterical woman… [I]t's relentless. If you speak out about sexism, she's pulling the sexism card. If you don't, you just have to sit there and take it. Which I do a lot of the time. If you do say something, you have to make sure you say it in a certain way so that they don't dismiss you as a hysterical woman, probably has her period. Believe me, women still face this and in politics, it is everywhere.' See Alice Sibley, 'The Changing Face of the Far Right,' *LSE Blog*, last updated 2 May 2023, https://blogs.lse.ac.uk/politicsandpolicy/the-changing-face-of-the-british-far-right.

83   'The stout and sometimes life-threatening resistance with which anti-Klan mobs met hooded demonstrations diminished the enthusiasm of Midwestern knights for continued confrontation,' Pegram, *One Hundred Percent American*, p. 180.

84   Ibid, p. 181.

85   'Occasional spasms of violence that accompanied the expansion of the hooded order into the North in 1923 and continued into 1925 were large-scale and public affairs, often involving

hundreds, even thousands, of brawling participants... In these riotous incidents, Klansmen often armed themselves and provoked confrontation by their unwanted gatherings in immigrant and Catholic districts, but organized and enraged opponents of the Invisible Empire inflicted most of the gunshot wounds, broken bones, and bloodied heads on outnumbered knights.' Ibid, p. 176. 'The Klan's bid to maintain an exclusionary Americanism advanced the development of pluralism by driving together, into anti-Klan coalitions, American cultural groups that had previously exhibited separate and even hostile relations. African Americans, Jews, some working-class groups, and isolated liberal white Protestants joined Catholics in demonstrations against the Klan... In 1923 "a crowd of negroes and whites," urged on by two local bankers who were officers in the Knights of Columbus, invaded a Ku Klux Klan meeting in Perth Amboy, New Jersey. In the Klan stronghold of Indianapolis, the American Unity League affiliate included African Americans, Jews, and Germans along with Irish Catholics. Italian musicians played "Wearin' o' the Green" in the 1923 St. Patrick's Day parade there. These temporary alliances did not dispel the tensions and animosities that had hampered relations between ethnic Catholics, blacks, Jews, and white Protestants into the 1920s, nor did they produce a fully functional multi-ethnic democracy.' Ibid, p. 87.

86   'The editor of the *Catholic World*, for example, warned in 1923 that if the Klan were allowed to persist and the state failed to protect Catholic citizens from its provocations, they would employ "self-defense, even to the extent of bloodshed..."' MacLean, *Behind the Mask*, p. 13. 'Full-scale riots by anti-Klan Catholics broke out in northeastern Ohio and in Massachusetts. Throughout 1924 and 1925, outdoor Klan meetings in the Bay State attracted mobs of angry opponents armed with guns and stones who waded into the hooded ranks. Brawls became a standard accompaniment of large Klan meetings there.' Pegram, *One Hundred Percent American*, p. 83. Today's international Christian alliances are far more unified around conspiracies of gender ideology, than they are at odds over religious preference.

87   See David J. Goldberg, 'Unmasking the Ku Klux Klan: The Northern Movement against the KKK, 1920-1925,' *Journal of American Ethnic History*, 15, no. 4 (1996) p. 32-48.

88   Ibid, p. 42.

89   'African-American newspaper editors spoke with some wariness and with more than a hint of cynicism about the sudden focus on the Klan. *The Cleveland Gazette* pointed out that Cleveland's mayor evinced little concern about the Klan until "Catholics and Jews were hit"; the Pittsburgh Courier noted that "no one objected to the crime of mob violence as long as the Negro was the victim"; and using markedly similar words, the *Chicago Defender* commented that "little attention was paid to these things when members of our group were the sole sufferers." Nevertheless, some African-American leaders welcomed the opportunity to work with Catholics and Jews in combatting prejudice.' Ibid, p. 37.

90   'An Open Letter to America on the Ku Klux Klan,' *The Messenger*, December 1920, access via marxists.org https://www.marxists.org/history/usa/pubs/messenger/v2nRN-12-dec-1920-Messenger.pdf

91   'Mob Violence and the Ku Klux Klan,' *The Messenger*, September 1921, access via marxists.org https://www.marxists.org/history/usa/pubs/messenger/1921-09-sep-mess-RIAZ.pdf.

92   Ibid.

93   'The Ku Klux Klan: How to fight it,' *The Messenger*, November 1921, access via marxists.org https://www.marxists.org/history/usa/pubs/messenger/1921-11-nov-mess-RIAZ.pdf

94   'Fact vs. Fiction,' *The Messenger*, June 1922, access via marxists.org, https://www.marxists.org/history/usa/pubs/messenger/06-jun-1922-mess-RIAZ.pdf.

95   Pegram notes, 'ordinary Klansmen often resented what one disgruntled Hoosier exalted cyclops, or lodge president, called "the hollering for money all the time ... and not using the principles which our men was sold upon,"' *One Hundred Percent*

American, p. 16.

96   Abbott Kahler, '"Murder Wasn't Very Pretty": The Rise and Fall of D.C. Stephenson', *Smithsonian Magazine*, last updated 30 August 2012, https://www.smithsonianmag.com/history/murder-wasnt-very-pretty-the-rise-and-fall-of-dc-stephenson-18935042.

97   Peter Amann has provided considerable historical detail on the development of the Black Legion, for example, which became a considerable force with 60,000 to 100,000 members (he calls this 'a conservative estimate') by the 1930s. As the civic fraternities of the second KKK dissolved this model of 'Vigilante Fascism' developed in its place. Robed in black cloak, the Legion developed 'night riding' as its signature action and concentrated on vigilantist intimidation, bombing and murder. It prospected a militarised fascist program of genocide and annihilation. By 1936, for example, there was a plan by leader Bert Effinger 'to kill One Million Jews by planting in every American synagogue during Yom Kippur time-clock devices that would simultaneously release mustard gas.' Amann, 'Vigilante fascism,' p. 512.

98   Especially physicians, who benefited from the coterminous rise in mainstream eugenics. See Jacqueline Antonovich, 'White Coats, White Hoods: The Medical Politics of the Ku Klux Klan in 1920s America,' *Bulletin of the History of Medicine*, 95, no. 4 (2021) p. 437-463.

99   'People just had no regrets; I really expected them to be confessional, regretful or embarrassed, or any of those kinds of things. And they really weren't.' Ko Bragg, 'First came suffrage. Then came the Women of the Ku Klux Klan,' *The 19th*, last updated 28 December 2020, https://19thnews.org/2020/12/first-came-suffrage-then-came-the-women-of-the-ku-klux-klan.

100   Anonymous, 'Black Middletown – W173,' interview by James R. Gardener (recorded July 1980), *Black Middletown Project*. Can be accessed online: https://dmr.bsu.edu/digital/collection/MidOrHis/id/373/rec/35.

101   Ibid.

102   Dr. Kenneth Davis, 'Oral History and Transcript,' interview by Warren Vander Hill (recorded January 2003), *Jewish Oral History Project II*. Can be accessed online: https://dmr.bsu.edu/digital/collection/MidOrHis/id/129/rec/4.

103   Rachel Lipp, 'Oral History and Transcript,' interview by Warren Vander Hill (recorded February 1979), *Jewish Oral History Project I*. Can be accessed online: https://dmr.bsu.edu/digital/collection/MidOrHis/id/75/rec/24.

104   Sister Jean Perry, 'Oral History and Transcript,' interview by Joseph Duncan (recorded June 2006), *Catholic Church Oral History Project I*. Can be accessed online: https://dmr.bsu.edu/digital/collection/MidOrHis/id/482/rec/51.

105   Lucie Williams, 'Oral History and Transcript,' interview by Hurley Goodall (recorded February 1972), *Black Muncie History Project*. Can be accessed online: https://dmr.bsu.edu/digital/collection/MidOrHis/id/58/rec/.

3. Moral Purity and the Suffragettes

1   Margaret Hunt, 'The De-Eroticization of Women's Liberation: Social Purity Movements and the Revolutionary Feminism of Sheila Jeffreys,' *Feminist Review*, no. 34 (1990) p. 25.

2   Sally Hines, 'Sex wars and (trans) gender panics: Identity and body politics in contemporary UK feminism,' *The Sociological Review*, 68, no. 4 (2020) p. 699-717. Accessed online: https://journals.sagepub.com/doi/10.1177/0038026120934684

3   Ibid.

4   The siege mentality of some gender critical writers blinds them to the power relations of their 'struggle'. Britain is on the front line of a battle against gender ideology, according to Dana Vitalosova: 'Just as at the beginning of the past century, when British women of the First Wave were grappling with the injustice of being denied the right to vote, women are now fighting the unfairness of being denied the freedom of thought and expression. Although women and feminists in many countries

are currently battling gender ideology, it is in the UK where the clashes seem most severe. A century ago, it was here the fight for women's suffrage took the most ferocious form.' Dana Vitalosova, 'Striking Similarities Between Treatment of Modern Gender Critical Feminists and British Suffragettes,' *4W*, last updated 25 March 2020, https://4w.pub/the-striking-similarities-between-the-treatment-of-modern-gender-critical-feminists-and-british-suffragettes.

5   Mallory Moore, 'Elite feminism and the reproduction of the social order,' *chican3ry*, last updated February 18 2022, https://chican3ry.medium.com/elite-feminism-and-the-reproduction-of-the-social-order-875227f52e.

6   Because antifascist organisers have fought to ensure there are consequences to their actions.

7   Sylvia Pankhurst, *The Suffragette Movement: An Intimate Account of Persons and Ideals* (London: Virago, 1977) p. 30.

8   Ibid, p. 40.

9   These groups, often competing with each other, remained on the margins of mainstream politics. They were solidly middle class and often connected to the Liberal party. Leading suffragists were the daughters and wives of MPs, university dons, bishops, industrialists, landowners and merchants. For a detailed history of the Church Congresses see Timothy W. Jones, *Sexual Politics in the Church of England, 1857-1957* (Oxford: Oxford University Press, 2013). Many of these women would go on to be key actors in suffrage. In the 1880s The Union of Women Workers, Mothers Union and Girls' Friendly Society, developed through the Anglican women's sections. The expansion of female clerical labour was also developing throughout Britain in the mid-century. As the threat of secularisation advanced, the Church of England prioritised the recruitment of voluntary woman lay workers, promoted feminine symbols of piety, along with new theses about the social roles of women as mothers, carers and beacons of morality. See Brian Heeney, 'The Beginnings of Church Feminism: Women and the Councils of the Church of England 1897-1919,'

The Journal of Ecclesiastical History, 33, no. 1 (1982) p. 89-109.

10   Anne Digby, 'Poverty, health and the politics of gender in Britain 1870-1948,' in Anne Digby and John Stewart (eds) *Gender, Health and Welfare* (Abingdon: Routledge, 2015).

11   Philippa Levine, *Victorian feminism 1850-1900* (London, Hutchinson Education, 1987) p. 72-3.

12   Suzanne Elisabeth Morgan, 'A passion for purity: Elice Hopkins and the politics of gender in the late-Victorian church' (PhD thesis, Bristol University, 1997) p. 58. Can be accessed on-line: https://research-information.bris.ac.uk/en/studentTheses/a-passion-for-purity-ellice-hopkins-and-the-politics-of-gender-in.

13   Judith R. Walkowitz and Daniel J. Walkowitz. '"We Are Not Beasts of the Field": Prostitution and the Poor in Plymouth and Southampton under the Contagious Diseases Acts,' *Feminist Studies*, 1, no. 3/4 (1973) p. 81.

14   Ibid, p. 83.

15   Ibid, p. 98.

16   Jim Jose and KCasey McLoughlin, 'John Stuart Mill and the Contagious Diseases Acts: Whose Law? Whose Liberty? Whose Greater Good?', *Law and History Review*, 34, no. 2 (2016) p. 251.

17   See Lisa Lowe's fourth chapter, 'The Ruses of Liberty' in her landmark book, *The Intimacies of Four Continents*. The chapter examines British colonial governance in India and China in the nineteenth century and includes a focus on Mill's ideas of liberty and empire. Lisa Lowe, *The Intimacies of Four Continents* (Durham: Duke University Press, 2015) p. 101-33.

18   Eileen Hunt Botting and Sean Kronewitter, 'Westernization and Women's Rights: Non-Western European Responses to Mill's Subjection of Women, 1869-1908,' *Political Theory*, 40, no. 4 (2012) p. 468.

19   John Stuart Mill, *On Liberty* (1859), econlib, can be accessed online as an ebook: https://www.econlib.org/library/Mill/mlLbty.html.

20   Ibid.

21   John Stuart Mill, *The Subjection of Women* (London: Long-mans, Green, Reader, and Dyer, 1869) Project Gutenberg. Can be accessed online as an e-book: at: https://www.gutenberg.org/files/27083/27083-h/27083-h.htm.

22   Judith Walkowitz, *City of Dreadful Delight* (Chicago: University of Chicago Press, 2013) p. 24.

23   Ibid, p. 82.

24   Judith R. Walkowitz, 'The Politics of Prostitution,' *Signs*, 6, no. 1 (1980) p. 126.

25   Judith R. Walkowitz, 'Male Vice and Feminist Virtue: Feminism and the Politics of Prostitution in Nineteenth-Century Britain', *History Workshop*, 13 (1982) p. 105.

26   Ibid, p. 105.

27   William Thomas Stead, 'Government By Journalism,' (1886) can be accessed via the Internet Archive: https://archive.org/details/GovernmentByJournalismWilliamThomasStead/page/n17/mode/2up.

28   For a review of 'new journalism' from a media historical perspective see, Kate Campbell, 'W. E. Gladstone, W. T. Stead, Matthew Arnold and a New Journalism: Cultural Politics in the 1880s,' *Victorian Periodicals Review*, 36, no. 1 (2003) p. 20-40. For another discussion of Stead and the 'personal journalism' style of the 'New Journalism' see Richard Salmon, '"A Simulacrum of Power": Intimacy and Abstraction in the Rhetoric of the New Journalism', *Victorian Periodicals Review*, 30, no. 1 (1997) p. 41-52.

29   Walkowitz, 'Male Vice,' p. 99.

30   Ibid, p. 85.

31   Gretchen Soderlund, *Sex Trafficking, Scandal, and the Transformation of Journalism, 1885-1917* (Chicago: University of Chicago Press, 2013) p. 35.

32   Walkowitz, 'Male Vice,' p. 84.

33   Morgan, 'A passion for purity,' p. 160.

34   Ibid, p. 116.

35   Ibid, p. 173.

36   Hopkins helped to set up working men's clubs where alcohol consumption was regulated rather than encouraged by
the brewers. Elice Hopkins, *Work Amongst Working Men* (New
York: T. Whittaker, 1884) p. 124. Can be accessed via the Internet Archive: https://archive.org/details/workamongstworki-
00hopk_0/page/n7/mode/2up?q=organs.

37   Elice Hopkins, *The Power of Womanhood; or Mothers and
Sons* (New York: E.P. Dutton& Company, 1889). Can be accessed online: https://www.gutenberg.org/cache/epub/16047/
pg16047-images.html.

38   Vron Ware, *Beyond the Pale: White Women, Racism and History* (London: Verso, 2015) p. 162.

39   Morgan, 'A passion for purity,' p. 167.

40   Pankhurst, *The Suffragette Movement*, p. 222-3.

41   Ibid p. 36.

42   Mary Davis, *Sylvia Pankhurst: A Life in Radical Politics* (London: Pluto Press, 1999) p. 32. We reference Davis' work on Sylvia
Pankhurst because it is often excellent and aids our argument.
However, we should also note that Davis has published articles in
which she promotes gender critical movements and arguments.
Such arguments represent the forms of radical left politics that
seek to blame both 'gender ideology' and 'identity politics' for
problems of disunity on the Left. The kind of arguments that we
challenge in our previous book and in this one. For a period, the
Morning Star platformed various transphobic 'sex based' rights
advocates including Davis. See Mary Davis, 'Gender and its relation to capitalism,' *Morning Star Online*, last updated 13 October 2017, https://morningstaronline.co.uk/node/41845. Mary
Davis, 'Why everyone feminist should be a socialist and why
every socialist needs to be a feminist,' *Morning Star Online*, last
updated 16 October 2021, 'https://morningstaronline.co.uk/
node/41845.

43   Margaret Ward, 'Conflicting Interests: The British and Irish Suffrage Movements,' *Feminist Review*, no. 50 (1995) p. 131.

44   Ibid.

45   Ibid, p. 134.

46   Katelyn Burns, 'The rise of anti-trans "radical" feminists, explained,' *Vox*, last updated 5 September 2019, https://www.vox.com/identities/2019/9/5/20840101/terfs-radical-feminists-gender-critical.

47   Ward, 'Conflicting interests,' p. 137.

48   Mary Davis, *Sylvia Pankhurst*, p. 37.

49   Adam Hochschild, *To End All War: How the First World War Divided Britain* (Oxford: Pan Books, 2012) p. 283-4.

50   Pankhurst, *The Suffragette Movement*, 'Introduction.'

51   June Purvis, 'Emmeline Pankhurst in the Aftermath of Suffrage, 1918–1928' in *The Aftermath of Suffrage: Women, Gender, and Politics in Britain, 1918-1945*, ed. Julie V. Gottlieb, Richard Toye (London: Palgrave Macmillan, 2013) p. 19.

52   Simon Webb, *Suffragette Fascists* (Barnsley: Pen & Sword History, 2020) p. 277-9.

53   Christabel Pankhurst quoted in Hochschild, *To End All Wars*, p. 279. While Christabel marched rightward, her former Irish comrade suffragettes would move on to join the nationalist women's organisation, Cumann na mBan and join the Easter Rising. Skeffington became founder of the Irish Women's Worker's Union during the 1913 Lockout and a pacifist, who organised supplies for the Easter Rising. See Margaret Ward, *Hanna Sheehy Skeffington: A Life* (Cork: Attic Press, 1997).

54   Purvis, 'The Aftermath of Suffrage', p. 24.

55   Hochschild, *To End All Wars*, p. 315. That's more than half a million pounds in today's money.

56   Webb, *Suffragette Fascists*, p. 205.

57   Hochschild, *To End All Wars*, p. 258-61.

58   Webb, *Suffragette Fascists*, p. 259. Christabel lost the election

nonetheless.

59   Purvis, *The Aftermath of Suffrage*, p. 20.

60   Hochschild, *To End All Wars*, p. 279.

61   Returning from her travels in North America, Emmeline had 'changed [her] views profoundly.' As she put it, after 'the [1926] general strike ... I saw that there were only two issues before the country, and that anyone who had the real interests of women at heart would stand firmly behind Mr. Baldwin [Stanley Baldwin, Tory Prime Minister] and the Government. I am now an Imperialist.' Interview in *Morning Post*, quoted in Purvis, *Aftermath of Suffrage*, p. 30-1.

62   Quoted in Davis, *Sylvia Pankhurst*, p. 97.

63   Editorial of the first issue of *The Woman's Dreadnought*, launched on 8 March 1914, International Women's Day. Can be accessed online: https://www.britishnewspaperarchive. co.uk/search/results/1914-03-08?NewspaperTitle=Woman%2527s%2BDreadnought&IssueId=BL%2F0002235%2F19140308%2F&County=London%2C%20England.

64   Groups like the North of England Society for Women's Suffrage had a more working class composition than other suffrage groups. These were mostly unionised factory workers, often involved in the Women's Trade Union League. Women textile workers from Northern England presented a petition to Parliament with over 37,000 signatures demanding women's suffrage. Mary Davis highlights the role played by working class women suffragists: 'In a remarkable refutation of the class prejudices of the established suffrage societies and the gender-blind myopia of the labour movement, these "radical suffragists" (notably Eva Gore-Booth, Sarah Reddish, Sarah Dickenson, Selina Cooper and others), consciously set about the task of forging an alliance between feminism and socialism.' Mary Davis, *Sylvia Pankhurst*, p. 18.

65   Sylvia Pankhurst, 'Women members of Parliament,' *Worker's Dreadnought*, 10, no. 39 (1923). Can be viewed online at the LSE Digital Library: https://digital.library.lse.ac.uk/objects/

lse:liq237muv.

66   This skewed moral reasoning and comparativism had other effects. Middle class suffragettes projected patriarchy onto male labour, rather than bourgeois men. This not only helped ratify the authority of patriarchal union representatives over labour, but completely obscured the agency of women workers, whom they represented as women needing moral rehabilitation. Similar attitudes emerged in the 1970s. Domestic violence against women was essentialised to working class men. Working class women victims were related to as helpless victims, requiring the aid of middle class women.

67   Jules Joanne Gleeson and Elle O'Rourke, *Transgender Marxism* (London: Pluto Press, 2021) p. 12.

68   Ibid.

69   Hochschild, *To End All Wars*, p. 369.

70   Julie Bindel, 'It's time to take a stand for civilisation', @bindelj, *X*, 22 October 2023, https://x.com/bindelj/status/1716208081955115421.

71   Mary Harrington, 'Israel's enemies are blinded by the sins of America: Pro-Palestinian Leftists offer no better alternative,' *Unherd*, last updated 18 October 2023, https://unherd.com/2023/10/dont-blame-israel-for-the-sins-of-america.

4. The British Union of Fascists and Fascist Feminism?

1   The same painting was recently targeted by activists from Just Stop Oil.

2   Julie V. Gottlieb, *Feminine Fascism: Women in Britain's Fascist Movement 1923-1945* (London: IB Tauris, 2000) p. 151.

3   Ibid, p. 164.

4   Quoted in Simon Webb, *Suffragette Fascists*, p. 294.

5   For more on Elam see this interesting testimony and explo-

ration from her granddaughter, Angela McPherson, 'A grandmother's legacy. The gift that keeps on giving?' *Women's History Review*, 30, no. 4 (2021) p. 688-700.

6   Stephen Dorril, *Blackshirt: Sir Oswald Mosley and British Fascism* (London: Penguin, 2007) p. 282.

7   Webb, *Suffragette Fascists*, p. 242.

8   Ibid, p. 293, 303.

9   Ibid, p. 168-9.

10   Dorril, *Blackshirt*, p. 282.

11   Quoted in Webb, *Suffragette Fascists*, p. 292-3.

12   Susan McPherson and Angela McPherson, 'The private and political journey of Norah Dacre Fox, a suffragette turned fascist,' *Women's History Magazine*, Issue 69 (Summer 2012) p. 14.

13   Webb, *Suffragette Fascists*, p. 165.

14   Webb, *Suffragette Fascists*, p. 211-2.

15   'A number of WAS members joined the British Union of Fascists.' Nina Boyd, *From Suffragette to Fascist: The Many Lives of Mary Sophia Allen* (Cheltenham: The History Press, 2013) p. 209.

16   Boyd, *From Suffragette to Fascist*, p. 156.

17   Webb, *Suffragette Fascists*, p. 335.

18   Boyd, *From Suffragette to Fascist*, p. 157.

19   Ibid.

20   Boyd, *From Suffragette to Fascist*, p. 134. She lost with only 6.5% of the vote.

21   Webb, *Suffragette Fascists*, p. 336.

22   Gottlieb, *Feminine Fascism*, p. 154.

23   Boyd, *From Suffragette to Fascist*, p. 284-5.

24   Gottlieb, *Feminine Fascism*, p. 298.

25   Ibid, p. 282.

26   Ibid, p. 310-1.

27   For more on Rotha Lintorn-Orman and the British Fascis-

ti, see Edward White, 'Conservatism with Knobs On,' *The Paris Review*, last updated 2 December 2016, https://www.theparis-review.org/blog/2016/12/02/conservatism-with-knobs-on. See also this episode of the excellent Bad Gays podcast about Lintorn-Orman's life, 'S7E10: Rotha Lintorn-Orman,' accessed online 30 September 2024, https://badgayspod.com/episode-archive/s7e10-rotha-lintorn-orman.

28   Martin Durham, 'Britain,' in *Women, Gender and Fascism in Europe, 1919-45*, ed. Kevin Passmore. (Manchester: Manchester University Press, 2003) p. 218.

29   BBC News, 'MI5 saved royal fascist from jail', *BBC News*, last updated 5 March 2006, http://news.bbc.co.uk/1/hi/england/norfolk/4775682.stm.

30   'In violent opposition to all this sphere of Jewish effort rise the schemes of the International Jews. The adherents of this sinister confederacy are mostly men reared up among the unhappy populations of countries where Jews are persecuted on account of their race. Most, if not all, of them have forsaken the faith of their forefathers, and divorced from their minds all spiritual hopes of the next world. This movement among the Jews is not new. From the days of Spartacus-Weishaupt to those of Karl Marx, and down to Trotsky (Russia), Bela Kun (Hungary), Rosa Luxembourg (Germany), and Emma Goldman (United States), this world-wide conspiracy for the overthrow of civilisation and for the reconstitution of society on the basis of arrested development, of envious malevolence, and impossible equality, has been steadily growing. It played, as a modern writer, Mrs. Webster, has so ably shown, a definitely recognisable part in the tragedy of the French Revolution. It has been the mainspring of every subversive movement during the Nineteenth Century; and now at last this band of extraordinary personalities from the underworld of the great cities of Europe and America have gripped the Russian people by the hair of their heads and have become practically the undisputed masters of that enormous empire.' See Winston Churchill, 'Zionism versus Bolshevism', *Illustrated Sunday Herald*, 8 February 1920, p. 5. Can be accessed online:

https://en.wikisource.org/wiki/Zionism_versus_Bolshevism.

31   Gottlieb, *Feminine Fascism*, p. 131.

32   Ibid.

33   As Gottlieb explains, 'during the BUF's East London campaign, anti-Semitism was one of the main planks supporting the women's platform. The whole discourse surrounding slum clearance was buttressed by reference to Jewish corruption and domination: "Fascism does not need the poisoned blood money of aliens to rehouse British people." [Anne] Brock Griggs spoke of the "evil force of finance, which flourishes as weeds do in the garden they destroy." At one of her meetings campaigning for the LCC elections, Brock Griggs spoke of corruption in housing, and argued that "when the Tories were in power, the head of the Housing Committee was a Jew – Levita, but 3 years ago when Labour came into office a great change took place, another Jew – Silkin was the head." BUF women contributed their voices to the movement's line of argument that only Jews should be conscripted for service as "British life and wealth must not be sacrificed in Palestine." In regard to the same issue, the BUF played on male fears of the alien's sexual licentiousness and threat to White women by claiming that "Jews are the international enemy, that Arabs are complaining that Jewish men are outraging Arab women in Palestine."' *Feminine Fascism*, p. 132.

34   Ibid, p. 131.

35   Webb, 'Suffragette Fascists,' p. 143.

36   Webb, 'Suffragette Fascists,' p. 231-2.

37   Oswald Mosley, *The Greater Britain* (London: Jeff Coats Ltd, 1934) p. 54. Can be viewed online at archive.org,

https://ia801403.us.archive.org/10/items/greater-britain-the-oswald-mosley_202206/Greater%20Britain%2C%20 The%20-%20Oswald%20Mosley.pdf.

38   Quoted in Gottlieb, *Feminine Fascism*, p. 102.

39   Gottlieb, *Feminine Fascism*, p. 117-8. See also Dorril, *Black Shirt*, p. 246.

40   Gottlieb, Feminine Fascism, p. 119.

41   Boyd, *From Suffragette to Fascist*, p. 237-8.

42   Gottlieb, *Feminine Fascism*, p. 155-6.

43   Anne Marie Waters, 'Women Erased: Emmeline Pankhurst,' *Anne's Substack*, last updated 6 May 2024, https://annemariewaters.substack.com/p/women-erased-emmeline-pankhurst.

44   Martin Pugh, 'Why Former Suffragettes Flocked to British Fascism,' *Slate*, last updated 14 April 2017, https://slate.com/news-and-politics/2017/04/why-the-british-union-fascist-movement-appealed-to-so-many-women.html.

45   This quote was sourced from the excellent substack on Ireland and fascism, *Black is the Light*. See: 'Norah Elam – Feminist, Animal Rights Activist, Fascist,' *Black is the Light*, last updated 26 December 2022, https://blackisthelight.substack.com/p/norah-elam-feminist-animal-rights.

46   Atwood, somewhat ambiguous on her position over contemporary 'gender wars', was able to recognise the 'obsessed' nature of the gender critical brain, when she was interviewed by transphobic then-*Guardian* journalist Hadley Freeman. See Josh Milton, '"Gender critical" journalist tries to grill Margaret Atwood on trans rights. It backfires, badly,' *Pink News*, last updated 19 February 2022, https://www.thepinknews.com/2022/02/19/margaret-atwood-hadley-freeman-trans-gender-critical.

47   Dorril, *Blackshirt*, p. 487.

48   Gottlieb, *Feminine Fascism*, p. 68, 70, 94.

49   Serena Bassi and Greta LaFleur, 'Introduction: TERFs, Gender-Critical Movements and Postfascist Feminisms,' p. 319.

50   Quoted in, Gottlieb, *Feminine Fascism*, p. 43.

51   Ibid, p. 69n.

52   Ibid, p. 106.

53   Lewis and Seresin, 'Fascist Feminism: A Dialogue,' p. 466.

54   Gottlieb, *Feminine Fascism*, p. 272.

55   Ibid, p. 148.

56   Ibid, p. 272.

57   Barbara Storm Farr, *The Development and Impact of Right Wing Politics in Britain, 1903-1932* (New York: Garland, 1987) p. 55.

58   Gottlieb, *Feminine Fascism*, p. 19-20.

59   Storm Farr, *The Development*, p. vi.

60   Gottlieb, *Feminine Fascism*, p. 16.

61   Beverly Bryan, Stella Dadzie, Suzanne Scafe, *The Heart of the Race* (London: Verso, 2018) p. 150.

62   Winifred Breines, *The Trouble Between Us*, p. 134.

63   Gottlieb, *Feminine Fascism*, p. 20

64   James Renton, 'The British Empire's Jewish Question and the Post-Ottoman Future,' in *The Jew as Legitimation: Jewish-Gentile Relations Beyond Antisemitism and Philosemitism*, ed. David Wertheim (Palgrave Macmillan: London 2017) p. 144.

65   See Satnam Virdee, *Racism, Class and the Racialized Outsider* (Bloomsbury: London, 2014). See also Richmond and Charnley, *Fractured*, chapter 4 for worker anti-alienism vs Jewish workers (p. 96-122) and chapter 5 for worker anti-alienism vs Black/Asian/Chinese workers (p. 123-49).

66   Gottlieb, *Feminine Fascism*, p. 104.

67   Lewis and Seresin, 'Feminist Fascism: a dialogue', p. 468.

68   Gottlieb, *Feminine Fascism*, p. 5.

69   Norah Elam, 'Fascism, Women and Democracy,' *Fascist Quarterly*, 1, no. 3 (July 1935) p. 290-8. A reproduction of this essay is found in *Fascist Voices: Essays from the 'Fascist Quarterly' 1936-1940* (London: Black House Publishing, 2019) p. 28-9.

70   Ibid.

71   Gottlieb, *Feminist Fascism*, p. 128-9.

72   'The Proclamation of the Irish Republic', *National Museum of Ireland*, accessed online 1 September 2024: https://www.museum.ie/en-IE/Collections-Research/Collection/Resilience/Artefact/Test-3/fb71e3dc-2e95-4406-bc46-87d8d6b0ae5d.   For the contribution of women to the Easter Rising see Liz Gillis

and Mary McAuliffe (eds) *Richmond Barracks 1916: We Were There: 77 Women of the Easter Rising* (Dublin: Four Courts Press, 2016).

73   Hanna Sheehy-Skeffington, 'Letter to Alice Park,' Dublin, Ireland, 25 February 1922 in Margaret Ward, *Hanna Sheehy Skeffington, Suffragette and Sinn Féiner* (Dublin: University College Dublin Press, 2018) p. 190.

74   Ward, *Hanna Sheehy Skeffington*, p. xvii.

75   Angela McPherson notes that despite becoming a British fascist, Elam was a 'lifelong Irish nationalist' and 'railed against the Black & Tans within my mother's earshot, reporting how she rejoiced whenever she heard one of them had been strung up to a lamp post,' 'A grandmother's legacy,' p. 691.

76   Ward Gahan, Naomi O'Leary, Mary McAuliffe, Tim McInerney, 'Transcript: Women in Politics,' *The Irish Passport*, accessed online 2 January 2025, https://www.theirishpassport.com/transcripts/transcript-women-in-politics/.

77   In particular, Cumann na mBan. See Margaret Ward's classic *Unmanageable Revolutionaries Women and Irish Nationalism* (London: Pluto Press, 1995). See also Sharon Furlong, '"Herstory" Recovered: Assessing the Contribution of Cumann na mBan 1914-1923,' *The Past: The Organ of the Uí Cinsealaigh Historical Society*, no. 30 (2009-2010) p. 70-93.

78   Mary, McAuliffe, 'The Treatment of Militant Anti-Treaty Women in Kerry by the National Army during the Irish Civil War,' *Éire-Ireland*, 58, no. 3 (2023) p. 76.

79   For a brilliant debate and contextualisation of this tragic split see Tommy Graham, in discussion with Síobhra Aiken, Leeann Lane, Mary McAuliffe and Margaret Ward, 'Sister against sister – women, the Treaty split and the Civil War', *History Ireland Podcast*, 15 May 2022, can be accessed at: https://www.historyireland.com/sister-against-sister-women-the-treaty-split-and-the-civil-war/.

80   Mary McAuliffe, 'You've heard of the Blueshirts but who were Ireland's Blue Blouses?,' *RTE*, 15 December 2023. Can be accessed

online: https://www.rte.ie/brainstorm/2023/1215/1422003-
ireland-blue-blouses-kathleen-browne-blueshirts-fine-gael. Interwar historiographies of fascism are complicated in the Irish
case because of a policy of Irish neutrality and the independent
strategic footings of the IRA. For an introduction see: Raymond
M. Douglas, 'Ailtiri Na hAiséirghe: Ireland's Fascist New Order,'
History Ireland, 17, no. 5 (2009) p. 40-4. See also, Raymond. M.
Douglas, 'The pro-Axis underground in Ireland, 1939-42', *Historical Journal*, 49, no. 4 (2006) p. 1155-83.

81   Mary McAuliffe, 'Doubts grow over "women in the home"
referendum', *Mastodon*, 2 September 2023, https://mastodon.
ie/@marymcauliffe/110995228955765292. For background to
the 'women in the home' debate in Ireland see Laura Cahill-
lane, 'According to Ireland's constitution, a woman's duties are
in the home – but a referendum could be about to change its
sexist wording,' *The Conversation*, last updated 1 February 2024,
https://theconversation.com/according-to-irelands-constitu-
tion-a-womans-duties-are-in-the-home-but-a-referendum-could-
be-about-to-change-its-sexist-wording-222477.

Conclusion

1   Stephanie E. Jones-Rogers, *They Were Her Property: White
Women as Slave Owners in the American South* (New Haven: Yale
University Press, 2019).

2   Terese Jonsson, *Innocent Subjects: Feminism and Whiteness*
(London: Pluto Press, 2020) p. 166.

3   Li Zhou, 'How 2022 became the year of the Latina Republican,' *Vox*, last updated 20 September 2022, https://www.
vox.com/the-highlight/23329428/latina-republican-candi-
dates-2022-red-wave.

4   Candace Owens, 'Nobody Wants to Talk About the Christian Holocaust,' interviewed by Piers Morgan, reposted by *ANCA
– Armenian National Committee of America*, YouTube, 18 June 2024,
https://www.youtube.com/watch?v=iWhaoQlEg0c&ab_chan-

nel=ANCA-ArmenianNationalCommitteeofAmerica.

5   Candace Owens, 'Israel Vs. Palestine with Norman Finkel-stein,' *Candace Owens Podcast*, 17 November 2023, YouTube, https://www.youtube.com/watch?v=te1y7ahp2LQ&ab_chan-nel=CandaceOwensPodcast.

6   Christopher Wiggins, 'After Iowa shooting, Candace Owens says LGBTQ+ community is "sexual plague on our society",' *Advocate*, last updated 5 January 2024, https://www.advocate.com/news/candace-owens-lgbtq-sexual-plague.

7   Norman Finkelstein, 'Transgender Cult,' *X*, 14 June 2023, https://x.com/normfinkelstein/status/1669001147456057348?l ang=en.

8   Russell Brand, 'Norman Finkelstein – on Oct.7 Attacks, Israeli Propaganda & Gaza,' *Stay Free Podcast*, 22 December 2023, https://www.podchaser.com/podcasts/stay-free-with-russell-brand-4912796/episodes/norman-finkelstein-on-oct7-att-195706053.

9   Vaca, *Evangelicals Incorporated*, p. 221.

10   Enzo Traverso, 'A fundamental pillar of classical fascism was anti-communism. (Mussolini defined his movement as "revolution against revolution".) There is nothing comparable in the postfascist imagination, which is not haunted by Jungerian figures of militiamen with metallic bodies sculpted in the trenches. It knows only bodybuilders trained in ordinary fitness centres. Communism and the left are no longer its foremost, mortal enemies, and it does not transcend the limits of a radical conservatism. In this postfascist mental landscape, the Islamic terrorist who has replaced the Bolshevik does not work in the factories but hides away in the suburbs populated by postcolonial immigrants.' Traverso, *The New Faces of Fascism*, p. 13.

11   See 'The Perpetual War: The Israeli Wager on Time with Abdaljawad Omar,' *Millennials Are Killing Capitalism Live!*, 12 September 2024, YouTube, https://www.youtube.com/watch?v=Zx8LS771Cu4&ab_channel=MillennialsAreKilling-CapitalismLive%21. For an analysis of the Resistance News

Network and the western denial of the rationality of national liberation actors in the Arab region see Tom Gann, 'Gaza is Free And Does Not Bargain,' *New Socialist*, last updated 12 July 2024, https://newsocialist.org.uk/gaza-is-free-and-does-not-bargain.

12   Benji Hart, Kelly Hayes, Jasmine, Stuart Schrader, Alex Vitale, 'Cop City is only the beginning, unless we fight,' *truthout*, audio recording and transcript, last updated 1 June 2023, https://truthout.org/audio/cop-city-is-only-the-beginning-unless-we-fight.

13   For more on Mumsnet's peculiarly British role in the growth of a national moral panic: Hannah Woodhead, 'Has Mumsnet become a hub of online transphobia?,' *Huck Magazine*, last updated 30 April 2018, https://www.huckmag.com/article/mumsnet-transphobia-online; Edie Miller, 'Why is British media so transphobic?,' *The Outline*, 5 November 2018, https://theoutline.com/post/6536/british-feminists-media-transphobic.

14   Gianluca Martucci, 'Pope Francis and Italian PM Meloni raise concerns over Italy's declining birth rate,' *Euronews*, last updated 13 May 2023, https://www.euronews.com/2023/05/13/pope-francis-and-italian-pm-meloni-raise-concerns-over-italys-declining-birth-rate.

15   Many on the left seem oblivious of Pope Francis' fetish for demography concerns. Michael Löwy sees only a 'Vatican with red flags', as featured on *Verso Blog*, last updated 9 February 2024, https://www.versobooks.com/en-gb/blogs/news/to-the-vatican-with-red-flags?srsltid=AfmBOopH2T59g8C5vfk-jX3cAnxG79l-mMgf41r5t5u99CMnAJzhBqUCN.

16   Georgia Meloni, 'President Meloni's speech at the Budapest Demographic Summit – "Family is the key to security" session', *Italian Government*, 14 September 2023, transcript can be accessed online: https://www.governo.it/en/articolo/president-meloni-s-speech-budapest-demographic-summit-family-key-security-session/23579.

17   Mitropoulos, *Contract and Contagion*, p. 49-50.

18   For background to the intergenerational histories of Ital-

ian interwar fascism, neo-fascism, and Fratelli d'Italia see David Broder, *Mussolini's Grandchildren* (London: Pluto Press, 2023).

19   Jules Gill-Peterson, 'The Cis State II', sadbrowngirl, last updated 3 June 2022, https://sadbrowngirl.substack.com/p/the-cis-state-ii.

20   Thanks to Mallory Moore for highlighting the US 'new feminist' connection to 'gender critical' movements in Britain. Mallory first documented the Bindel-Lahl connection here: Mallory Moore, 'From as early as 2016, Julie Bindel was doing collaborative activist work with Christian conservative Jennifer Lahl of the religious "bioethics" group CBC,' @ Chican3ry, X, 3 May 2022, https://twitter.com/Chican3ry/status/1521403606737563648?t=ar-xMlHAARAAFkNZtvA-GOw&s=19. Lahl has also been on panels with other anti-trans hate groups who operate with charity status, such as Gary Powell of LGB Alliance. See Vic Parsons, 'Activist instrumental in the launch of the LGB Alliance linked to anti-abortion and anti-LGBT+ hate groups,' *Pink News*, June 2020, https://www.thepinknews.com/2020/06/03/lgb-alliance-gary-powell-center-bioethics-culture-alliance-defending-freedom-anti-lgbt.

21   Mary Harrington, 'What is King Charles hiding?,' *UnHerd*, 8 May 2023. https://unherd.com/2023/05/what-is-king-charles-hiding.

22   Andrew Brown, 'Mary Harrington interview: the failure of liberation,' *Church Times*, last updated 17 March 2023, https://www.churchtimes.co.uk/articles/2023/17-march/features/features/mary-harrington-interview-the-failure-of-liberation.

23   Ibid.

24   Luke Turner was sued at the High Court for libelling Power and Miller. Power and Miller garnered gender critical and far right support and nearly thirty thousand pounds in donations to fight their case. But Turner won. The case has bankrupted both Miller and Power and forced their private WhatsApp messages and online racism into public view. See Luke Turner, 'Victory in High Court libel case against Nina Power and Daniel "DC"

Miller,' *luketurner.com*, last updated November 8 2023, https://luketurner.com/victory-in-high-court-libel-case-against-nina-power-and-daniel-dc-miller.

25   See Luke Turner, 'Nina Power,' *luketurner.com*, last updated 2 July 2 2024, https://luketurner.com/Nina_Power.

26   Ibid.

27   Linda Stupart, 'On trauma, paranoia, and fascism (and on Nina Power),' *The White Pube*, last updated May 4 2019, https://thewhitepube.co.uk/texts/2019/on-trauma/.

28   Danny Kruger is the former speech writer of David Cameron (and came up with the infamous 'Hug a Hoodie' canard). He is now a leading intellectual of the 'New Conservatism' family within the Tory party. This group is racist, restrictionist, critical of some parts of the neoliberal consensus and commits to a pro-natalist restoration of Britain. Kruger and New Conservative co-chair Miriam Cates have recently set up the 'New Social Covenant', a think tank. On the front page it reads, 'We need to recover the concept of the household economy, the oikos, to enable a more integrated life with flexible work closer to home. This will help both men and women balance the commitments to family, community and employment.' See *New Social Covenant*, accessed 24 September 2024, https://www.newsocialcovenant.co.uk/family.

29   Nina Power, 'After the Individual,' *National Conservatism*, 15 May 2023, YouTube, https://www.youtube.com/watch?v=Mut1etJkVD8&ab_channel=NationalConservatism.

30   Theodor W. Adorno, *Prisms* (Cambridge: MIT Press, 1997) p. 30.

31   Power, 'After the Individual'. Italics are our emphasis.

32   Sandra Duffy, 'Bell v Tavistock on Appeal: Court of Appeal Upholds Young Persons' Ability to Consent to Puberty-Blocking Medication,' *Oxford Human Rights Hub*, last updated October 5 2021, https://ohrh.law.ox.ac.uk/bell-v-tavistock-on-appeal-court-of-appeal-upholds-young-persons-ability-to-consent-to-

puberty-blocking-medication/.

33   Power, 'After the Individual'.

34   The philosopher Christa Peterson has done a lot of work to analyse and publicise such connections. 'In her new book, *The Economist's* Helen Joyce claims the trans "global agenda" is "shaped" by three Jewish billionaires. The sourcing is vague in the book, but she has previously cited Jennifer Bilek. Bilek has previously cited an explicit Nazi. Gendercrit launders antisemitism.' @Christapeterso, *X*, 18 July 2021, https://x.com/christapeterso/status/1416599964214448130?lang=en.

35   Gleeson and O'Rourke, *Transgender Marxism*, p. 22.

36   Jordy Rosenburg, 'The Daddy Dialectic,' *LA Review of Books*, 11 March 2018, https://lareviewofbooks.org/article/the-daddy-dialectic.

37   Harrington offered a series of less than cryptic tweets. 'The uniparty hate the English,' @moveincircles, *X*, 3 August 2024, https://x.com/moveincircles/status/1819815666435895736?t=e6uKFH7WZY_wCmfyoam7k-w&s=19. See also 'Mothers for Remigration,' @moveincircles, *X*, 3 August 2024, https://x.com/moveincircles/status/1819649962411516096?t=-oDc8x_bzUtv97oy-gSi3w&s=19.

Louise Distras, gender critical songwriter: 'According to Keir Starmer "I'm a far right thug" because I care about women + girls.' See Billy Bragg, 'Don't expect to hear much condemnation from those gender-criticals,' @billybragg, *X*, 5 August 2024, https://x.com/billybragg/status/1820491985934807221?t=EF-dthq4Z1wfolW5hhUT9NA&s=1.

Kellie Jay-Keen (aka Posie Parker): 'It's a riot if it's about your own country but a legitimate peaceful protest if it's about a country half way across the world,' @ThePosiePark-er, *X*, 2 August 2024, https://x.com/ThePosieParker/status/1819285414202556586?t=MzHMKkjKezO2otpabRvX-1w&s=19.

Meanwhile, another group of GC activists felt the need to put out a statement, writing 'We, the undersigned, are deeply disturbed that populist messages particularly targeting Muslims have gained traction among significant numbers of social media accounts associated with the gender critical movement'. They believe that their movement must not associate with 'anyone who justifies or incites the violent scapegoating of immigrants and minoritised communities'. They later add: 'Many of us did not anticipate that this would ever need saying, or that the gender critical movement would ever face a serious incursion from the far right... We are not prepared to accept the hard work done by so many being co-opted and endangered by people inciting and defending race riots.' This sense of a progressive self-identity puts this gender critical group above ideology. It means that at all times one's ideas are 'captured' or 'incorporated' by the far right not that were already commensurate with and historically co-constitutive of it. 'Statement on the gender critical movement and the far right,' *GC Anti Far-Right*, last updated 13 August 2024, https://gcantifarright.wordpress.com/2024/08/13/statement-on-gc-movement-and-the-far-right.

38   Langston Hughes, *Tired*. Can be accessed: https://genius.com/22601839/Langston-hughes-tired/Arent-you-for-the-world-to-become-good-and-beautiful-and-kind-let-us-take-a-knife-and-cut-the-world-in-two-and-see-what-worms-are-eating-at-the-rind.

Acknowledgements

For Breya and Thea, our little comrades, we learn from you every day. Keep reminding us of the different ways we can say *no*. Teach us to think with that cartwheel that says not today because I'm cartwheeling. And that singing that says not today because I'm singing. Love to my family for all their support over the years. I'm lucky to have grown up into generations of communists where we could rethink how to be communists. Nat I'm so lucky to have met you, my best mate, my love.

To our intersex liberation marxist, trans-anarchist, trans-marxist, trans-rogue, and antifascist feminist comrades we are in this with. To all those who've reminded us how to betray this messed up world. There is no reconciliation with the wrong world so we will live it wrongly. Nobody is free until we all are free. Palestine will be free.

Alex Charnley

For Caleb, the best comrade I could ever have dreamt of. You have brought such immense joy into our lives.

Thank you to my family and friends, above all to Alexandra for continuing to hang out with me and for always having my back.

For my trans and feminist comrades, and all others steadfast in the struggle against patriarchy, colonialism and fascism.
Free Palestine.

Michael Richmond

www.ingramcontent.com/pod-product-compliance
Lightning Source LLC
Chambersburg PA
CBHW031152020426
42333CB00013B/624